PRAISE FOR BACH AT LEIPZIG

"The most substantial play based on classical music since Peter Shaffer's *Amadeus* . . . [Moses] has taken a single moment of history . . . and from it spins a tale of competition, intrigue, betrayal, folly, and an overwhelming passion for music. Moses's most impressive achievement here is the perfect balance between the serious stuff of this play—human ambitions and inevitable shortcomings—and its medium, splendid comedy frothing at every level[, and] it is *Bach at Leipzig*'s deft structure, continual plot surprises, emotional accuracy, and delicious and unstinting humor that will captivate future audiences."   —Barbara Adams, *Ithaca Times*

"Moses . . . may be some kind of genius . . . [*Bach at Leipzig*] has many brilliant moments."

—Joe Adcock, *Seattle Post-Intelligencer*

"A remarkably silly yet intellectually stirring comedy . . . Reaches for an ineffable beauty and mystery that is hard to shake."   —Tom Keogh, *Queen Anne News*

"One of the best-conceived, best-crafted new plays I have seen."   —Neil Novelli, *The Post-Standard*

"The erudite young Moses [is] a clearly gifted writer."

—Misha Berson, *The Seattle Times*

ELIOT KHUNER

ITAMAR MOSES

𝔅𝔞𝔠𝔥 𝔞𝔱 𝔏𝔢𝔦𝔭𝔷𝔦𝔤

Itamar Moses' work for the stage includes the full-length plays *Outrage, Bach at Leipzig, Celebrity Row,* and *The Four of Us;* the one-act plays *Authorial Intent* and *Idea;* and the book for the musical *The Hook.* His work has been produced and work-shopped regionally by the Wilma Theater, Milwaukee Repertory Theatre, the Hangar Theatre, Florida Stage, ACT Seattle, Portland Center Stage, the American Conservatory Theatre, and the McCarter Theatre, and developed in New York by the Manhattan Theatre Club, the Underwood Theatre, New York Theatre Workshop, New York Stage and Film, HERE Center for the Performing Arts, and La Mama Etc. His monologue *Good Apples* was published in *Monologues by Men for Men* by Heinemann Press, and his ten-minute play *Men's Intuition* was published in *Take Ten II: More Ten-Minute Plays* from Vintage. Moses has received new play commissions from Playwrights Horizons, Berkeley Repertory Theatre, the Wilma Theater, and the Manhattan Theatre Club. He holds an M.F.A. in dramatic writing from New York University, has taught playwriting at Yale and NYU, and is a New York Theatre Workshop Usual Suspect. Born in 1977 in Berkeley, California, he now lives in Brooklyn, New York.

Bach at Leipzig

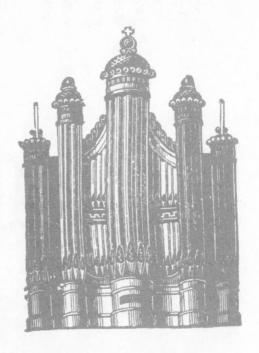

Faber and Faber, Inc.

An affiliate of Farrar, Straus and Giroux

NEW YORK

Bach at Leipzig

A PLAY BY

Itamar Moses

WITH A PREFACE BY
TOM STOPPARD

FABER AND FABER, INC.
An affiliate of Farrar, Straus and Giroux
19 Union Square West, New York 10003

Copyright © 2005 by Itamar Moses
Preface copyright © 2005 by Tom Stoppard
All rights reserved
Distributed in Canada by Douglas & McIntyre Ltd.
Printed in the United States of America
First edition, 2005

Library of Congress Control Number: 2005926650
ISBN-13: 978-0-571-21111-1
ISBN-10: 0-571-21111-9

Designed by Gretchen Achilles

www.fsgbooks.com

1   3   5   7   9   10   8   6   4   2

For my father, Gavriel, who is everywhere in this play
And for my mother, Yael, who is everywhere outside of it

Acknowledgments

This play, like all plays, benefited from collaborators whose questions, advice, and encouragement were indispensable. Kevin Moriarty and the Hangar Theatre took a chance on the play very early, as did Lou Tyrrell, Des Gallant, and Florida Stage. It is not an exaggeration to say that the lessons of those first two productions changed me as a writer forever. Of course, those theaters might never have read the play at all without the generous advocacy of Garrett Eisler and Johnathan McClain. Crucial early notes on the text came from my classmates and teachers in the Graduate Dramatic Writing Program at Tisch, and also from Michelle Tattenbaum, whose dramaturgy demands sense, and from Tess Taylor, whose sense demands truth. Jim Nicola, Toni Amicarella, and New York Theatre Workshop supported the play during its transition from old to new versions of itself. Liz Timperman, Mark Linn-Baker, and New York Stage and Film assembled a ridiculously talented cast that expanded my sense of possibility, and led me to Bob Boyett, a producer whose genuine love of theater is an inspiration. Joe Hanreddy, Paul Kosidowski, and the amazing resident acting company at Milwaukee Rep gave me a chance to see, fully realized, what this long journey had produced. Almost every step along the way was aided and abetted by the incomparable Mark Christian Subias. And, finally, I am grateful to have found in Pam Mackinnon, my director and friend, someone who knows how to fight for what a play needs, who is a joy in rehearsal, and who never stops working until the house lights dim on opening night: "Where are we?"

Preface

My qualifications for occupying this space are meager. Thanks
to the Wilma Theatre in Philadelphia, where we each were to
have a play in the 2004/5 season, Itamar Moses and I shared a
platform one evening and then a train back to New York. The
experience easily overcame my resistance to reading casually
encountered scripts. When we parted, I was carrying a copy of
Itamar's Wilma play—not, as it happens, *Bach at Leipzig*, but
Outrage.

Reading *Outrage* converted me. *Bach at Leipzig* is, as far as
I remember, the only play-in-typescript I have ever solicited
from an author, and I was not disappointed. The first and most
pleasing thing about it was that it was so different from *Outrage*, and both plays seemed equidistant from the main models
of young American theater. Of course, the two plays exhibited
the common characteristics of a wordsmith with a ludic
streak, and of those, what was most striking to me, and what
pleases me more than the innumerable sly witty lines, are the
plays' sly, witty structures. *Bach at Leipzig*, for example, mimics
in form its own subject matter.

At the time of reading I was at my most amenable to writing a few encouraging lines for an "unknown" playwright. The

balance has shifted since then: my acquaintance with Itamar's plays has remained where it was—two read, none seen. Since then, his reputation has rippled out from a handful of productions, and I suspect that I am already too late to "introduce" Itamar Moses; so let this stand merely as a thank-you note to the Wilma for introducing *me* to *him*, a new and original voice in the American theater.

TOM STOPPARD
JUNE 2005

Bach at Leipzig

Production History

Bach at Leipzig was originally produced at The Hangar
Theatre in Ithaca, New York, in July 2002, and further
developed in productions at Florida Stages in Manalapan,
Florida, in December 2002, and at New York Stage and Film
Company at Vassar College in Poughkeepsie, New York, in
2004.

The play had its New York premiere on November 14,
2005, at the New York Theatre Workshop (James C. Nicola,
artistic director, and Lynn Moffat, managing director), under
the direction of Pam MacKinnon; sets were designed by
David Zinn; costumes by Matthew J. Lefebvre; lights by
David Lander; sound by John Groma; and fight direction by
Felix Ivanov. The production stage manager was Carol Clark.
The cast was as follows:

JOHANN FRIEDRICH FASCH	Boyd Gaines
GEORG BALTHASAR SCHOTT	Michael Emerson
GEORG LENCK	Reg Rogers
JOHANN MARTIN STEINDORFF	Jeffrey Carlson
GEORG FRIEDRICH KAUFMANN	Richard Easton
JOHANN CHRISTOPH GRAUPNER	David Schramm
THE GREATEST ORGANIST IN GERMANY	Himself

Cast of Characters

JOHANN FRIEDRICH FASCH, *organist, and Kapellmeister at Zerbst, fifties.*

GEORG BALTHASAR SCHOTT, *organist at the Neuekirche in Leipzig, fifties.*

GEORG LENCK, *organist, and Kantor at Laucha, late thirties.*

JOHANN MARTIN STEINDORFF, *organist, and Kantor at Zwickau, twenties.*

GEORG FRIEDRICH KAUFMANN, *organist, and Kantor at Merseburg, fifties.*

JOHANN CHRISTOPH GRAUPNER, *organist, and Kapellmeister at Darmstadt, fifties.*

THE GREATEST ORGANIST IN GERMANY, *organist, and Kantor at Hamburg.*

SETTING: The Thomaskirche, Leipzig, Germany, 1722. Later, 1750.

AUTHOR'S NOTE: In spite of the highly constructed plotting, the archness of the language, the period setting, and so on, all of which seem to lend themselves to a heightened and distancing style of performance, this play works best when inhabited as fully and realistically as possible. My experience has been that when the temptation to "perform" takes over, not only does the play lose emotional resonance but it actually becomes less funny. Play it "for real."

Act One

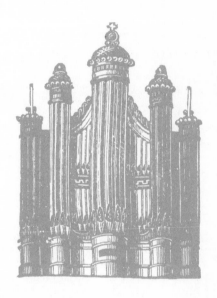

One

*(As the lights fade, the beginning of Bach's "Prelude in A Minor"
for organ plays, perhaps cutting off with the sound of wind, a
carriage, a slamming door. At this, a man in his fifties,* JOHANN
FRIEDRICH FASCH, *appears, alone in a pool of light, wearing a
traveling cloak.)*

FASCH

Leipzig. June, 1722.

My darling Anna:

By the time you receive this letter, I will have sent it. I
know that I embarked suddenly, my sweet angel. I am sorry
for it, especially so soon after the birth of our infant
daughter, so soon that she does not yet have even a name.
But I had no choice.

From an early age, my gingersnap, I heard everything
in nature—from the squeak of wheels on a passing
stagecoach to the slap of feet in mud puddles—as melodies
and harmonies. The insomnia that has plagued me since
childhood is, I think, in part a result of the hum that often
springs, unbidden, from my throat. As is the insomnia that
now plagues *you.* Eager for the training I knew I needed, I
found my way here, to Leipzig, and to the man whose
reputation drew me: Johann Kuhnau. He held the post of
Thomaskantor, presiding over both the services at the
Thomaskirche and the students at the Thomasschule,
which stood across from each other on the Thomaskirchof,
in the area of Leipzig honoring St. Thomas.

Recognizing my potential, Kuhnau began to give me

private lessons in his study. It became clear to me then how profound was his devotion to the Lutheran faith. On his walls, above his writing desk, his washbasin, *everywhere*, he had affixed scrolls bearing the sayings of Martin Luther. Above his keyboard, one, my favorite, read: "Youth should be taught this art, for it makes fine, skillful people." And indeed it was not simply as a musician but as a person that Kuhnau instructed me, alternating musical lessons with religious ones. Music, Kuhnau taught me, was God's gift to us, and our only worthy way of praising God in return. And at the close of every lesson he would say, "You, Johann, are my most cherished pupil."

But, Anna, my meadow, my lamb, as I grew older I found it in me, as never before, to *disagree* with Kuhnau. About composition, at first, as I tired of the rigid forms he taught me. But soon my queries, like our lessons, shifted from music to religion. Need our music praise God *at all*? I wondered. Why not make it simply for each other? Soon, I found myself questioning even the most fundamental tenets of his faith. Consubstantiation! Election! The Doctrine of Predestination itself! Each meeting would begin with humble apologies for the last but soon escalate to bitter argument. And one day when I went to his study for my lesson, bearing a *gift*, no less, that day—oh, Anna, my empath, this will break your heart—that day there was another student in his room. A new student at his keyboard. And he said, Anna—I heard it myself—Kuhnau said to this boy, "You, Johann, are my most cherished pupil."

I dropped my gift by the door, where it shattered. It had been ridiculous in any case: a simple vase, unadorned. I left the school that very night. My teacher and I never spoke again. And my insomnia, which his devotion had quelled, returned. Then I met you, my milk-skinned moppet, and it was conquered for good. When your doctor procured for me that mysterious powder from the East. But I remained . . . haunted.

Which brings me to the reason for my sudden flight. The night I left you, I received a missive. It bore the unmistakably genuine seal of the Leipzig Guild of Musicians, and was enfolded in the metal case they employ for important correspondence. Inside was a letter. Or, no, not a letter but a piece of music, a melody that, when decoded, contained a message. "I am dying," he said. "I wish to choose a replacement. Come see me at once." Such melancholy! For here was terrible news, and yet, in the same moment, a chance to reconcile! And more! A chance to guide Leipzig according to my principles! For what else could this mean? *He must have seen that he was wrong!* I pounded roadways into dust, threw coins at gatekeepers, pausing only in the courtyard itself, where, through the windows of the church, I could hear the inimitable sound of my old teacher at the organ. I mounted the steps, entered the church, and stalked the halls to the great doorway itself . . .

(FASCH *turns.*)

Two

(Lights up on the anteroom of the Thomaskirche.)

(Double doors upstage center lead into the church proper. Various other exits, archways. Several simple wooden benches stand against the stone walls. Another man in his fifties, GEORG BALTHASAR SCHOTT, *is seated here, near the doors. A moment.)*

SCHOTT Johann Friedrich Fasch!

FASCH Georg Balthasar Schott.

SCHOTT What brings you here?

FASCH Stagecoach, primarily. And, for this last portion, my feet.

SCHOTT Of course. And for what reason have you come?

FASCH It is a beautiful church. One doesn't come to Leipzig without paying a visit to the Thomaskirche.

SCHOTT Indeed, indeed. But no, Herr Fasch. Why are you *here* at all? In Leipzig?

FASCH A whim, Georg. I am simply passing through. *(Beat.)* Although I might ask you the same question.

SCHOTT You might, but it would be strange. I live here.

FASCH No: *here.* Are you not still employed as organist at the Neuekirche? In the cobbler's district, under the bridge, across town?

SCHOTT I am. But there is a problem with the organ at the Neuekirche.

FASCH What's that?

SCHOTT It is across town, under the bridge, in the cobbler's district.

FASCH Ah.

SCHOTT Strange time for a journey all the way from Zerbst. Travel is dangerous. War is brewing between the cities of Merseburg and Zwickau.

FASCH The roads are quiet. Merseburg has just appointed a new ambassador to Zwickau, to secure the peace. (*Pause.*) From the courtyard I could have sworn I heard *him* playing.

SCHOTT So you did. He is engaged in a closed and lengthy concert for himself.

FASCH How unusual.

SCHOTT Not at all. It is his custom every afternoon. For hours.

FASCH What a boon for those who live nearby! They must listen enraptured!

SCHOTT Indeed, they *must*. It's audible for half a mile. At the tavern across the street, the hired musicians abandon their efforts, as Kuhnau fills the rafters above their heads and renders them obsolete.

FASCH I hear nothing now.

SCHOTT An acoustic anomaly. His music escapes through the stained glass on the other side of the cathedral, and those nearby are entombed in silence. But it is, as you heard, perfectly clear from a greater distance.

FASCH (*Privately.*) Oh, yes. I remember.

SCHOTT Of course. You were his student.

FASCH Yes.

SCHOTT So perhaps you are *not* simply passing through after all.

FASCH Perhaps not simply. No. (*Pause.*) Speaking of which . . .

(FASCH *gestures for* SCHOTT *to let him pass.* SCHOTT *stares back innocently.*)

SCHOTT What?

FASCH May I go?

SCHOTT You may. It was delightful to see you.

FASCH May I go *inside*?

SCHOTT Oh no, no, no! He is loath to relinquish a single moment at the instrument while he can still play!

FASCH Of course. But how can we be sure that he plays still?

(SCHOTT *opens the door a crack. There is a sudden swell of pipe-organ music, in mid-phrase, a rapid-fire run of high notes over low groans. He closes the door again, and the music snaps off as suddenly as it began.*)

SCHOTT He does.

FASCH He's . . . remarkable. After all these years.

SCHOTT Yes. All these years.

FASCH What is he—seventy-five, eighty?

SCHOTT Eighty-one.

FASCH Eighty-one. Remarkable. (*Pause.*) Do you think he's nearly finished?

SCHOTT I can only hope that he is.

FASCH Perhaps if I could just call out to him, so that—?

(SCHOTT *opens the door a crack. There is another swell of music, even more impressive than the first.* FASCH *is rendered inaudible.*)

SCHOTT (*Over the music.*) What? I'm sorry, my friend, I can't hear you!

(FASCH *motions for* SCHOTT *to close the door. He does. The music snaps off.*)

SCHOTT You see? To make such an attempt now would do no good. You would raise your voice in greeting, and be drowned out by the many other voices under his command. You are too cavalier, Herr Fasch. It is a lucky thing that I am here, as a bulwark. To guard him.

FASCH Let me pass.

SCHOTT No.

FASCH It is not your place to forbid my entrance.

SCHOTT Nor is it yours to enter. Given your betrayal of all that he holds dear.

FASCH I . . . beg your pardon?

SCHOTT It is not mine you ought to beg. Your deviation from the good Lutheranism practiced by great men like Herr Kuhnau has thrown your congregation into utter disarray.

FASCH I am beloved in Zerbst.

SCHOTT I think not, Johann.

FASCH I assure you, Georg. You have confused me with another musician.

SCHOTT That seems unlikely.

FASCH It is *very* likely. Half the musicians in Germany are called Johann. The other half are called Georg. It is a blessing, Balthasar, that we all have middle names with which to distinguish ourselves from one another.

SCHOTT I suppose, Friedrich, that it is.

FASCH I shall wait until he emerges. Out of respect for *him*.

SCHOTT Very wise.

FASCH Do you think we might listen, from the threshold, as he plays?

SCHOTT I suppose.

FASCH You don't think he'll mind?

SCHOTT I don't think he'll notice.

(SCHOTT *opens the doors. The music flares.* FASCH *and* SCHOTT *stand in the open doorway, watching. At its peak, the music cuts off abruptly. Then it starts again, spasmodically. Then there is a thump, and a blare of adjacent low notes, as though the organist had pressed his head against the bottom of the keyboard and left it there. Which, judging from their reaction, is precisely what has happened. The drone sustains.*)

(FASCH *runs inside.* SCHOTT *backs away from the door, stunned.* FASCH *emerges.*)

FASCH There are clergy in the courtyard. Get them. (*Pause.*)
   Get them!
SCHOTT Yes. Yes. Right away.

(SCHOTT *runs off and can be heard offstage shouting.*)

SCHOTT Help! *Help! We need help!*

(FASCH *turns out, into a pool of light. The drone sustains quietly underneath.*)

FASCH But, Anna, the instrument he played is all that I
   have left of him now. I had hoped to return to you right
   away, my lily, my lake, but that is not possible. For
   something awful has occurred.
      I'll write again when I have time.

                                        Yours, *Johann*

(FASCH *releases a pigeon and watches it ascend: the sound of wings . . . wind . . .*)

(*Blackout.*)

Three

(GEORG LENCK, *late thirties, alone in a pool of light.*)

LENCK

Leipzig. June, 1722.

My dear Catherina:

I have arrived safely, and in time, having arranged passage with a gentleman who allowed me to accompany his carriage. Because he did not know I was there. Clinging to the underside of it. Yes, as I am fond of saying, I, Georg Lenck, am so poor that I cannot afford even a middle name with which to distinguish myself from other Georgs! But that, after all, is why I've come—to reverse my fortunes at last. And not through some foolhardy scheme, as when I had you defraud your parents by feigning an expensive illness called bogus fever. No. This time there is real glory to be had! I have brought with me dozens of letters in praise of my musical talent, and, thanks to my adept calligraphy, each is in a different script. And each signed by a fictitious duke. For this memorial is to be hosted by the Leipzig Council itself, the very men charged with selecting Kuhnau's replacement. This is indeed a happy day!

(LENCK *turns. Lights up on the anteroom.* FASCH *and* SCHOTT *are here.* LENCK *is sobbing on* FASCH's *shoulder.* FASCH *comforts him.*)

FASCH Georg Lenck. How wonderful of you to come.

LENCK There was no question about it, Herr Fasch. The moment I received the messenger pigeon bearing news of his demise, I knew that I would feel incomplete if I let him pass without paying tribute.

FASCH I trust that the trip from Laucha was uneventful.

LENCK I wish it had been. A crazed bandit accosted me on the road: dirty rags, a gleaming sword, a hood concealing his face. He tried to steal my luggage.

FASCH No.

LENCK Oh, yes.

FASCH It must have been dreadful.

LENCK No, it is very attractive, which is no doubt why he wished to steal it.

FASCH Well, we are very sorry to hear it.

LENCK Thank you. But it could have been worse.

SCHOTT Yes, there are things we'd be sorrier to hear. Your music, for example.

LENCK Excuse me?

SCHOTT For example, he might have stolen your music.

LENCK Ah. Hello, Herr Schott.

SCHOTT Lenck.

(SCHOTT *and* LENCK *shake hands.*)

LENCK Fear not. To prevent just such a calamity, I keep my scores inside my cloak, strapped to my very body. Indeed, the north is in utter disarray. *War* is brewing between Merseburg and Zwickau!

SCHOTT So I've heard.

FASCH Has not Merseburg just appointed a new ambassador to secure the peace?

LENCK No, they appointed a new ambassador to *fail* to secure the peace. Merseburg's prince has intentionally selected his least qualified subject.

SCHOTT Did you take my ring?

LENCK What? Oh. Yes. (*He returns a ring he obtained during the handshake.*) A keyboardist's fingers—if I don't keep them busy, they busy themselves.

SCHOTT Yes, you keep them *so* busy—at cards, and dice, and *worse*—that you spend more time in a cell than you do at the organ.

LENCK I am beloved in Laucha! (*To* FASCH.) Be careful with this one, Fasch. It is his habit to twist the truth about his rivals as a form of leverage.

FASCH I had noticed, yes.

LENCK When I was last in Leipzig auditioning for a post, at the Neuekirche, he suggested that we pool our resources and petition to *share* it. Then, the night before the audition, he slipped a note under my door, summoning me to a clandestine meeting at which he blackmailed me!

SCHOTT Auditioning for a post, Georg? I thought you were here to pay tribute.

LENCK (*Beat.*) So! By the time word of Kuhnau's death reached me, rumor held that he had collapsed while performing.

FASCH The deacons wouldn't allow us to move him until the doctor arrived. But by then, of course, it was too late.

LENCK It's true?

FASCH His music and his life, ending together, without the benefit of a cadence. A sudden and final interruption, of both the man and his art.

SCHOTT It was dramatic in the extreme.

LENCK The moment must have been.

SCHOTT No, the noise. His head depressed the keys. We had to listen to those sustained notes for half an hour. The man performed his own dirge with his face.

LENCK Sounds awful.

SCHOTT It certainly did. Kuhnau's features were so smooth, you see, it was hideously dissonant. If he'd had a sharper nose, narrower cheekbones—

FASCH Yes, Herr Schott, I'm sure that when you expire face-first into a keyboard your hawklike countenance will produce a glorious fugue.

SCHOTT Thirds, at least. It might have been thirds.

LENCK *(Moving toward the doors.)* The service is inside?

SCHOTT No.

FASCH Only the body.

LENCK *(Beat.)* I'm sorry. So he's all *alone?*

FASCH I . . . *(Beat.)* What do you mean?

SCHOTT The official memorial is to take place later on. For directly concerned parties only.

FASCH Ah, yes. Music. Eulogies. Food and drink.

SCHOTT Prayer.

LENCK And will you both attend?

FASCH I was his most cherished pupil. And he: my only teacher.

LENCK *(To SCHOTT.)* And yours as well? You being a native of the city?

SCHOTT As it happens, no. I chose, instead, to learn music from my father. But we were colleagues, of course. Peers.

LENCK *(Hiding his disappointment.)* Well . . . as an . . . *indirectly* concerned party I suppose that *I* must pay homage . . . now. *(Pause.)* He won't wait forever.

FASCH Quite.

SCHOTT Although, in fact, he will.

(LENCK opens the doors. Faint sad organ music floats out.)

LENCK Who do you suppose is playing? Quite an honor, to accompany Kuhnau's . . . final public appearance.

SCHOTT No one even asked me.

FASCH Nor me.

LENCK Well. Perhaps a harpsichordist is stretching.

(FASCH *and* SCHOTT *precede* LENCK *through the doors.* LENCK *claps* SCHOTT *on the shoulder as he passes, skillfully removing a gold chain from* SCHOTT'*s neck. He turns out, into a pool of light, with a smirk.*)

LENCK Catherina, things are on the turn. I promise you. And this time I really mean it. I'll write again when I have time.

Yours, *Georg*

(LENCK *releases a pigeon.*)

(*Blackout.*)

Four and Five

(Two men, in separate pools of light: GEORG FRIEDRICH
KAUFMANN, *who is in his fifties, and* JOHANN MARTIN
STEINDORFF, *who is in his twenties.)*

KAUFMANN Leipzig.
STEINDORFF June, 1722.

KAUFMANN
    My dearest Gisela:
        I hope this letter finds you well, and that you do not
    despise me for leaving you all alone, with our fair city on
    the brink of war, and only your gardener, valet, and
    footman to keep you company. I will try not to stay away
    long, though the footman, especially, has assured me that
    you will be in good hands. And though circumstances in
    Merseburg are precarious, my hope is to prevent bloodshed
    there, even while in attendance here.
STEINDORFF My dearest Susanne: *(Beat.)* No. My
    darling Henrietta: *(Beat.)* No, no. Maria, Magdalena,
    and Margaret, my minxes: *(Beat.)* No, no, no. *(Then,
    soberly.)*
    My dear father:
        Thank you, once again, for this chance at glory. As you
    said, though our fair city is on the brink of war, I am more
    likely to honor you here, at the keyboard, than there, with
    my sword. And I shall bring honor to you, Father. And to
    all Zwickau. As you command.

(Lights up on the anteroom. KAUFMANN *and* STEINDORFF *turn in.)*

KAUFMANN Truly, Johann, you must reconsider.

STEINDORFF I'm sorry, Georg, I cannot.

KAUFMANN Our presence here together is surely an opportunity! On your soil, and on ours, negotiations have failed. Where better to make one last attempt than on the neutral ground of Leipzig?

STEINDORFF Herr Kaufmann, I know that you take seriously your recent appointment as Merseburg's ambassador. But *I* am here solely in my capacity as a musician. I am not empowered to negotiate.

KAUFMANN Yours is the most powerful family in Zwickau, Herr Steindorff. That carries responsibilities you cannot avoid.

STEINDORFF *(Quietly.)* Yes, I know. *(Beat.)* But as I'd very much like to attend this memorial *before*—

KAUFMANN Martin, please. My people do not want a war.

STEINDORFF They ought to have considered that before they began bombarding Zwickau with missives, insulting my father.

KAUFMANN I beg your pardon. Those came in response to slanderous epistles from *your* city, insulting our prince. Furthermore, from what I have seen *all* of the letters— from *both* sides—are signed by entirely fictitious dukes! Have you considered that we may be the victims of a conspiracy by some tiny warmongering faction?

STEINDORFF No, for each letter is in a different script.

KAUFMANN Perhaps it is the work of a single adept calligraphist!

STEINDORFF Ridiculous. And, whether the letters are genuine or not, the rift they describe is all too real.

KAUFMANN Both our cities are Lutheran!

STEINDORFF Yes, but ours is determined to remain that way. Your prince allows bastardized cults to flourish! The Calvinists! The Pietists! All manner of unacceptable distinct sects! There is no hope of reconciliation.

KAUFMANN Then why have I repeatedly been invited to stay as a guest on your family's estate?

STEINDORFF Your understanding of politics is as nuanced as your music.

KAUFMANN Why, thank you!

STEINDORFF A halfhearted show of diplomacy is the final step toward open war.

KAUFMANN Your father is a lover of music, is he not?

STEINDORFF I . . . What of it?

KAUFMANN I heard that once there was an organist who owed him an *enormous* sum, but so taken was he with the man's skill at the keyboard that he never collected the debt.

STEINDORFF (*Overlapping.*) Yes, yes, but I fail to see—

KAUFMANN Think! *That* is what unites us! Our art! Our theatre! Our music! *Culture*, Steindorff! That is, in the end, all that distinguishes us—

STEINDORFF (*Wearily.*) From the animals, yes.

KAUFMANN No! From the English!

STEINDORFF What?

KAUFMANN From the Italians! From the rest of Europe!

STEINDORFF (*Beat.*) German culture is all that distinguishes us from non-Germans.

KAUFMANN Yes! And I propose a renewed commitment to our common Germanity! These sects are not irreconcilable, for they are not so distinct, after all!

STEINDORFF They are irreconcilable because they are almost exactly the same. The Doctrine of Predestination is the cornerstone of them all. But we Lutherans can accept the notion that an Elect few are Predestined for Paradise only if it comes with the private understanding that *all* of us are included. The Calvinists have made the small mistake of taking the same religion and imposing actual *standards*. Where they reign, they ban song, and dance, and all forms of expressing the very culture *you* so revere. The strictures they impose close like a vise from without! Limiting all freedom! Meanwhile, sprouting like weeds from within, the Pietists embrace an *individual* spirituality that frees them from all limits! Both are disaster.

KAUFMANN You simply parrot your father's rhetoric, Martin. And *he* longs for a time that may never return.

STEINDORFF Is that so?

KAUFMANN Yes. The very beginning of religion. When all of us were simply Lutheran.

STEINDORFF (*Beat.*) I'm going inside.

(LENCK *enters, followed by* FASCH.)

LENCK We'll join you.

KAUFMANN Wonderful!

STEINDORFF Ah, the insufficient prince.

LENCK Shouldn't you be opportunistically performing?

FASCH Steindorff played during the viewing of the body.

KAUFMANN How marvelous!

STEINDORFF Thank you. I do believe that I was.

KAUFMANN You know, gentlemen, I feel that I must admit: I am engaged in *researching* each and every one of you! Collecting old letters, interviewing acquaintances, reconstructing your lives!

FASCH To . . . what end, Herr Kaufmann?

KAUFMANN My hope is to assemble these findings into an exhaustive musical biography of our era. So, forgive me, but I do not know when I will ever again have the privilege of being among so very many fine composers!

(SCHOTT *enters. He takes in the occupants of the room.*)

SCHOTT Oh, my dear God.

FASCH Good morning, Balthasar.

SCHOTT Yes, we'll see. Gentlemen! Welcome to Leipzig! I
am happy that you have all been so warmly received by
our city.

STEINDORFF Hardly. When I arrived, a wild brigand of some
sort leaped from the bushes and attacked me on the road,
near the gates.

LENCK Was he wearing nothing but rags, and a hood, and
waving a sword?

STEINDORFF The very one! I've never been more convinced
of the wisdom of tucking my musical scores into the soles
of my boots, as I do when I travel.

(*During this*, SCHOTT *has moved to stand between the others and
the door.*)

SCHOTT But . . . before we go inside . . .

FASCH Oh, honestly, have you an *obsession* with blocking
this doorway?

SCHOTT You misunderstand. In fact, Fasch, I wish to . . .
(*Generally.*) First, in the sight of those gathered, composers
all, I am sorry if, in my protective zeal, I prevented you
from speaking to your teacher one last time.

FASCH Well. Well. I do appreciate it. In fact, perhaps I should
apologize for my behavior during that encounter as well.

SCHOTT Accepted.

FASCH All that remains now is to ensure that his legacy is
carried on as he would have wished.

SCHOTT Yes! My feelings exactly! Perhaps together we can
bring that about.

FASCH (*Offering his hand.*) Yes! Yes, to ensure that German
music—

SCHOTT *(Taking it.)* Remains exactly the same!

FASCH Yes. What?

STEINDORFF Touching.

LENCK Beautiful. Let's go in.

FASCH *(Blocking the door.)* Just a moment. Again, I apologize. However, he would have wanted nothing of the kind.

SCHOTT I beg your pardon, but I spoke to him daily for half my life.

FASCH And, begging yours, let me suggest that I think perhaps he altered in his final days.

SCHOTT I am so sorry. But why on earth do you think that?

FASCH He wanted music to survive, and would never have robbed it of the one thing it requires in order to do so.

SCHOTT And what is that, pray tell?

FASCH Innovation!

SCHOTT God forbid. Kuhnau prized good craftsmanship, yes, but never *innovation*.

FASCH Only because he often mistook innovation for poor craftsmanship.

SCHOTT Why should we obey the shifting fashions of the day? Or, worse, *set* them!

FASCH In the music! Only in the music, Herr Schott!

SCHOTT But when you deny the musical principles laid down by our predecessors you risk denying their religious ones as well.

FASCH That is preposterous! New music might, in fact, *reach* those who do not *like* the work of our predecessors. Or such would be the intent.

SCHOTT I am not comforted, Friedrich, for intent is not the issue.

KAUFMANN Me?

FASCH My middle name is also Friedrich.

KAUFMANN How strangely inconvenient.

LENCK Is this going to go on much longer?

STEINDORFF Yes, the memorial won't wait forever.

LENCK Although, in fact . . . (*Beat.*) No, he's right, it won't.

(FASCH *and* SCHOTT *block the doors together.*)

FASCH ⎤
⎬ Gentlemen!
SCHOTT ⎦

FASCH This should be of grave concern to you all.

SCHOTT Indeed, it should.

(*They turn back to each other.*)

FASCH Martin Luther did not nail his ninety-five theses to the great doors at Wittenberg only to have *you* rid the world of music.

SCHOTT Nor did he only to have *you* rid it of God! (*Beat.*) When the theme rises in a joyful figuration, it must be because the congregation, at that moment, sings of an angel's joy at the birth of our Lord. If the melody grows morose, it is at the turn of the story to Mary's grief as Christ lay dying, or because the word "sin" or "death" has cropped up in the text. And if we abandon these rules we will write music that brings the heart to *any* joy, or to joy at *anything*. To joy without God.

FASCH You sound just like him.

SCHOTT Why, thank you.

FASCH *Individuals* gravitate toward individual expressions of faith.

SCHOTT (*With contempt.*) So, you are a Pietist.

FASCH My point exactly! Why must everything have a name?

SCHOTT So that we know which houses to burn.

FASCH If a man feels his connection to the Eternal through pure music that brings pure feeling, then it is the godliness in it that matters! Not that someone sings the word

"God"! Form is an illusion! A fragile vase no sooner questioned than shattered! Why insist that *our* rules harden into permanence when no others ever have?

SCHOTT Because we got them right!

FASCH But when you give people the choice—

SCHOTT But, Fasch! It is *choice* that is the illusion! Life, like music, involves choice *only* on the part of the Creator! Why, that was the entire purpose of the Reformation!

FASCH What.

SCHOTT The Doctrine of Predestination!

FASCH Predestination is nonsense! It renders all our actions meaningless. The gates of heaven do not open at the capricious behest of some unseen hand. No! We seize the handle ourselves!

(The escalation has been steady. Now everyone stares at FASCH. *A long moment.)*

SCHOTT So. It is not *only* music you wish to alter. After all. *(Pause.)* And so what would become of the flock you'd lead as Kuhnau's successor?

FASCH Well, I . . . *(Long pause.)* I am not Kuhnau's successor.

SCHOTT Ah. But that is why you are here, is it not? *(Generally.)* That is why all of you are here? Not to *honor* the man but to *replace* him?

FASCH Someone must.

SCHOTT And clearly it must not be you. Mysticism is not faith! We are not meant to experience *pure feeling!* This is not Italy! Would you have us, as they do, drive our congregants into an unending sensual frenzy?

STEINDORFF Which way to Italy?

SCHOTT This is not a joke! Germany is in utter disarray— scattered bands of dukes and princes sprouting like weeds and turning on one another! And all the while the

Catholics close like a vise from without! Risen from the Mediterranean, an Italian ogre rattles the gates, roaring Vivaldi! To the southwest are poised a gaggle of French dances! And across the water our own Georg Friedrich produces opera after opera for the English!

KAUFMANN I am not across any water.

FASCH He means Handel. Whose name also begins with Georg Friedrich.

KAUFMANN How—

SCHOTT And do not think that this threat is confined to music or to politics. French cathedrals resplendent with gold and jewels! Drug-addled Italians painting the Son of God in whore's colors as some twisted grotesque! I do not know what they will call this ignominious new age, but it runs entirely counter to the spirit of the Reformation.

But. Just as this can infect our music, so too can our music beat it back. And Leipzig shall be our bulwark. But who among you is worthy to lead this great defense? Who will slay the ogre, crush the dancers, and preserve the old way anew? *Who will stand upon our battlements and lead us?*

(SCHOTT *turns away from the others brusquely and opens the doors. Music, once again, floats out. A moment.*)

SCHOTT It's all right. A cat is walking across the keyboard.

(SCHOTT *goes inside.*)

KAUFMANN I'm sorry. They're holding auditions for Kuhnau's post?

(FASCH *has removed a vial of white powder from his coat, pinches a bit between his fingers, and inhales it.*)

STEINDORFF (*Intrigued.*) What is that, Fasch?
FASCH It's medicinal. (*Beat.*) Gentlemen, shall we?

(*The lights shift.* KAUFMANN *and* STEINDORFF *turn out together.*)

STEINDORFF And now, Father, it is time.
KAUFMANN I'll write again, Gisela, when I have time.
STEINDORFF

Yours, *Johann*

KAUFMANN

Yours, *Georg*

(STEINDORFF *and* KAUFMANN *release pigeons together: two sets of wings.*)

(*Blackout.*)

Six

(A man in his fifties, JOHANN CHRISTOPH GRAUPNER, *alone, in a pool of light. He wears a traveling cloak.)*

GRAUPNER

Leipzig. June, 1722.

Doctor Schultz:

Throughout my journey from Darmstadt, I spoke aloud to myself the optimistic incantations you suggested. "I am important to those who are important to me." And: "I am beloved by those whose love matters." But they were empty in my mouth, and, at last, after hundreds of repetitions, the carriage driver begged me to be quiet.

I know, and you have repeatedly assured me, that I, Johann Christoph Graupner, ought to count myself lucky to have such a name and reputation. Which is to say, a name so recognizable that many people think they have heard of me, without being quite sure, and a reputation as the second-greatest organist in Germany. But my hope is that here, at last, it shall be different. That I shall surpass my nemesis, and be the most revered of all. My devotion to Calvinism allows me to accept nothing less.

To that end, I arranged my audition through letters, and contrived to delay my arrival until the day before the auditions were to begin, to build the anticipatory dread of the others, who would no doubt have noticed my conspicuous absence, and superstitiously avoided even the mention of my name. So that I would appear first as a more shadowy and menacing figure, I tarried near the gates until dark. At which point I was attacked by a daft highwayman, who emerged from the foliage. It is for this very reason that, when I travel, I attach my scores to the flesh of my thighs with surgical thread.

In any event, once inside the gates I descended upon the Thomaskirchof, seized a clergyman, and asked where I might find the others. Learning they'd taken quarters in the church itself, I mounted the steps, wrapped in my most impressive cloak, and lurked just outside the antechamber until I heard voices. I then pounded on the door, so that the echoing crashes might silence their conversation and better prepare them to witness their approaching doom . . .

(Lights up on the antechamber, as GRAUPNER *sweeps triumphantly into it. There is no one else in the room.)*

GRAUPNER Behold! *(Beat.)* Damn.

*(*GRAUPNER *hefts his luggage and stalks off deeper into the church.* STEINDORFF *enters from another direction holding a note. He is agitated. Seeing no one, he looks off in several directions. He rereads the note.* SCHOTT *enters. A moment.)*

STEINDORFF What is the meaning of this? A note, slipped under my door, summoning me to a clandestine—
SCHOTT Yes, Herr Steindorff, I was hoping to have a word.
STEINDORFF *(Thoughtfully.)* "Cantankerous."
SCHOTT I was hoping to have a word with *you.*
STEINDORFF Be my guest. But I am not so easy to describe in a word as you are.
SCHOTT I wish to discuss our agreement.
STEINDORFF I don't. I don't wish to be seen with you at all. The others could walk in at any moment.
SCHOTT Fear not. They've all gone to the tavern across the street.

STEINDORFF Even so. When the Council awards me the post tomorrow, the choice must appear untainted. And, in return for your aid, you will receive what you were promised: dominion over the students at the Thomasschule. There is nothing to discuss.

SCHOTT Oh, but there is.

(SCHOTT *produces a letter from his coat.*)

STEINDORFF What's that?

SCHOTT I have a younger brother in Zwickau. Perhaps you know him? Johann?

STEINDORFF Perhaps. What is his name?

SCHOTT That *is* his name.

STEINDORFF Oh! I thought—

SCHOTT Yes. He is the sub-deacon at your church.

STEINDORFF What does he do there?

SCHOTT He administers to the sick and the poor.

STEINDORFF Then, no. I do not know him.

SCHOTT Very well. But he knows you. He has seen you, after your performances on Sundays, stealing into the choir balcony.

STEINDORFF It's true, I go there when I wish to feel closer to God.

SCHOTT With a young lady.

STEINDORFF She wishes to feel closer to God as well.

SCHOTT I am sure. But which one?

STEINDORFF (*Perplexed.*) Which God?

SCHOTT No, which lady? On ordinary Sundays, it is Henrietta. On festival Sundays, it is Susanne. And on feast days, a trinity: Maria, Magdalena, *and* Margaret!

STEINDORFF (*Incredulous.*) What sort of Lutheranism does your brother practice?

SCHOTT Highly observant.

STEINDORFF No doubt.

SCHOTT In fact, most egregiously of all, it seems the newly appointed ambassador of Merseburg has *also* been your victim!

STEINDORFF *(Outraged.)* He has not!

SCHOTT *(Patiently.)* In that you have dallied with his wife.

STEINDORFF Oh, yes, I see.

SCHOTT I hold here a letter detailing these transgressions. And I am prepared to address copies to all who might find it of interest.

STEINDORFF Then I will have it dismissed as a forgery.

SCHOTT It bears the unmistakably genuine seal of the Leipzig Guild of Musicians.

STEINDORFF Then I shall blame the interference of a mischievous courier.

SCHOTT I will enfold it in the metal case we employ for important correspondence.

STEINDORFF But you are a Lutheran! Blackmail violates your principles!

SCHOTT And lechery yours. Punishing the latter seems to necessitate the former. For you, too, are a Lutheran.

STEINDORFF Exactly! Thus any sinful actions on my part were Predestined by God himself at the beginning of time. I had no choice!

SCHOTT I . . . Predestination is not an excuse to act badly! On the contrary, we *recognize* the elect by their good actions!

STEINDORFF Balthasar, perhaps you yourself seldom enjoy the company of a woman. If so, *I* can arrange for you a most pliant—

SCHOTT I seldom enjoy the company of a woman because my wife is dead. Taken in childbirth, along with our first child. *(He turns to go.)* Consider this divine judgment, Martin. For your crimes.

STEINDORFF Herr Schott. *Please!*

SCHOTT I have no choice. *(Pause.)* Unless . . .

STEINDORFF Unless?

SCHOTT Leave Leipzig.

(STEINDORFF *sits, defeated. Then he begins to laugh.*)

SCHOTT *Laughter*, Steindorff?

STEINDORFF My father embarked on this collusion because
he saw in you a kindred spirit. One who recognized the
threat to our faith and hoped to keep this post in our
hands. But you are not so righteous as you pretend.

SCHOTT Oh?

STEINDORFF No, you are nothing but a petty malcontent
salving his own wounds. Despite the way you have
anointed yourself the guardian of Kuhnau's legacy, in fact,
he *despised* you.

SCHOTT What do you mean? We were *peers*, colleagues—

STEINDORFF Yes, so long as you remain under the bridge, in
the cobbler's district—

SCHOTT I love the Neuekirche!

STEINDORFF Even when you were a boy! A native of
Leipzig! A musician! And yet never even admitted to the
Thomasschule!

SCHOTT I never applied!

STEINDORFF And if I abandon my claim? What then? You
cannot sway the Council on your own. Indeed, it was *you*
who first described their fractiousness! Some require
bribes, you said, and *we* supplied them! Some seek to
divine Kuhnau's final wishes, you said, and *we* confirmed
that he left none! Some seek the candidate with the most
fame, you said, and *we* persuaded Hamburg to double the
salary of its Kappelmeister to prevent him from attending!
Your knowledge was *useless* until we provided our
resources!

SCHOTT And so thank goodness your resources have already
been provided.

STEINDORFF *(Beat.)* But . . . ! I . . . !

SCHOTT Do you see now? The Greatest Organist in
Germany is conspicuously absent. My devotion to Kuhnau
is well known. I placed your bribes. The outcome is
inevitable. Goodbye, Martin.

(SCHOTT *walks away.*)

STEINDORFF *(Desperately.)* My father, you know, has
illegitimate children all over his estate. Once, among the
peasants on our land, there was a wheelwright. A rumor
in our house held that his eldest son was a bastard
Steindorff.

SCHOTT *(Beat.)* What on earth are you talking about?

STEINDORFF I asked my father, could we not take the boy
in? My father thought me soft. Unworthy of the Steindorff
name. He banished this wheelwright. Forced him to
uproot his family. To *show* me. You see?

SCHOTT Is that true?

STEINDORFF Almost heartbreaking, isn't it?

SCHOTT Yes. Almost.

STEINDORFF Though I'd willingly trade lives with that boy
now. *(Beat.)* But this post. This post, Herr Schott, is my
opportunity to *prove* that I . . . *(Pause.)* Your letter may or
may not have its intended effect. But if I simply leave, as
you ask, the result is a certainty: never again will I be
welcome in his house.

SCHOTT Nor will you if you disgrace it. *(Beat.)* I only mean:
you may try to earn his name and sully it instead. Which
prospect frightens you more?

(Pause. STEINDORFF *simply looks at* SCHOTT.*)*

SCHOTT So be it. I will release the bird tonight.

STEINDORFF I was wrong.

SCHOTT What about?

STEINDORFF Cantankerous is not strong enough. Not at all.

(The two men look up toward a sudden bustle of entrance.
LENCK, FASCH, *and* KAUFMANN *hurry into the room.)*

LENCK Gentlemen! Here you are!

SCHOTT Here we are.

FASCH *(To* STEINDORFF *and* SCHOTT.*)* My friends, we
thought you might like to join us.

LENCK I've brought cards. We are all going to gamble.

FASCH We are not.

SCHOTT *(With a glance at* STEINDORFF.*)* Yes, we are. All
of us.

LENCK There, you see? Splendid!

KAUFMANN Herr Schott, I was astonished to discover that
there is a tavern across the street from this church.

LENCK Kaufmann, there is a tavern across from the
Badenkirche in Merseburg!

KAUFMANN Oh, no. It looks like a tavern, but it is in fact a
repair shop for musical instruments. There were a number
of disagreements between myself and my musicians on the
subject, but it turns out that they go there, you see, to
have their strings tightened . . . when the tuning—

LENCK They told you it was a *music* shop? What's it called?

KAUFMANN The . . . ah . . . *(Pause.)* The Wench and Swine.

LENCK Who did you think the Wench and the Swine
were?

KAUFMANN The . . . the *owners.* A husband and wife who
operate the business together, with two separate
workshops, they told me, to complete repairs more
quickly! He works downstairs, and she upstairs, with
different . . . specialties . . . oh God . . .

SCHOTT *(With a look back at* STEINDORFF.*)* Upstairs at our
tavern, Herr Kaufmann, there is nothing but a pigeon loft.

FASCH How do the musicians play afterward?

KAUFMANN *Better*, actually.

FASCH Better how?

KAUFMANN With less urgency.

(SCHOTT, FASCH, *and* KAUFMANN *are gone, these last remarks fading.* STEINDORFF *lingers, lost in thought.* LENCK, *who trails a bit behind the departing throng, turns back toward him.*)

LENCK Come along, Steindorff. I have prepared a mug especially for you.

STEINDORFF Herr Lenck? May I have a moment?

LENCK You may. But do not dally long.

STEINDORFF May I have a moment with *you*?

LENCK Ah. Well. To take your own moments is your prerogative, but to lay claim to mine as well strikes me as greedy.

STEINDORFF Nevertheless.

LENCK (*A slight bow.*) I am at your service.

STEINDORFF I wish to discuss your debt.

LENCK (*Beat.*) You will have to be far, far more specific. I owe more than one. Forgive me.

STEINDORFF If I were to forgive you, you would owe one less. I refer to the debt you owe my father.

LENCK Which one?

STEINDORFF (*Perplexed.*) Which father?

LENCK No, which debt? I have admired him for so long that I am indebted to him for many things: his wisdom, his goodness, his upright—

STEINDORFF Your monetary debt.

LENCK Ah.

STEINDORFF Incurred over the course of an ill-fated night of card-playing at his estate.

LENCK This *is* beginning to sound familiar.

STEINDORFF In the amount of four hundred and thirty florins, eighteen groschen, and nine pfennig—

LENCK Yes—

STEINDORFF And also several horses and oxen.

LENCK Yes, yes, my memory has been sufficiently refreshed. What of it?

STEINDORFF He wants it repaid.

LENCK But . . . he said he was so taken with my skill at the keyboard that he—

STEINDORFF Nevertheless.

LENCK Your father well understands my circumstances.

STEINDORFF Indeed he does. More than once, he has remarked, "Georg Lenck is so poor that he cannot even afford a middle name, with which—"

LENCK Ah. He has stolen my joke. In fact, each of us now owes the other. Perhaps we ought simply to cancel both debts.

STEINDORFF My father wants his money.

LENCK He assured me that I would have *years*.

STEINDORFF You *have* had years.

LENCK Yes, but I assumed he meant *more* years.

STEINDORFF No. And if you are unable to pay, he will have no choice . . . but to imprison you.

LENCK I see. Or?

STEINDORFF (*Beat.*) He will imprison you.

LENCK Well, that's hardly a choice at all, is it?

STEINDORFF What shall I tell him?

LENCK Tell him . . . tell him that he needn't worry. For I am soon to marry into a wealthy family, and that if he gives me only a little more time—

STEINDORFF Ah. Do you refer to Catherina Kirkendale?

LENCK I . . . why yes, how—?

STEINDORFF I have an uncle in Laucha. A philosopher. Perhaps you know him? Georg?

LENCK Perhaps. What is his name?

STEINDORFF (*Beat.*) In any event, he assures me that you are in no way eligible to marry Fraulein Kirkendale; that, in fact, your presence in her chambers is the scandal of the town; and that, most damningly of all, upon each visit from her aging parents she forces you to adopt a masquerade wherein you disguise yourself as a nursemaid called Bodenschatz.

LENCK (*Incredulously.*) What sort of philosophy is it that your uncle practices?

STEINDORFF Morally relativistic.

LENCK No doubt.

STEINDORFF If you are unable to repay with coins, you can do so with labor. Yes, several years of indentured servitude on my father's land should—

LENCK No! (*Pause.*) Martin, *please.*

STEINDORFF I have no choice. (*Pause.*) Unless . . .

LENCK Unless?

STEINDORFF Leave Leipzig.

(LENCK *sits, defeated. Then he begins to laugh.*)

STEINDORFF (*Quickly, wearily.*) Yes, yes, I am not so righteous as I pretend, and so on.

LENCK (*Beat.*) What?

STEINDORFF And there is one further thing you must do for me. (*Correcting.*) For *him.*

LENCK What's that?

STEINDORFF Circumstances in Zwickau are precarious. As I am sure you are aware.

LENCK Of what?

STEINDORFF That there is a war brewing.

LENCK (*Beat.*) Is there? I had no idea.

STEINDORFF Pushed to the brink by a heated exchange of provocative letters.

LENCK A . . . heated exchange of provocative letters?

STEINDORFF Some of which publicize claims about my family that are as outlandish as they are damaging. Why, some of these so-called revelations even involve myself!

LENCK (*Perplexed.*) No, they don't. (*Then, quickly, covering.*) Do they?

STEINDORFF Yes. And *you* must rob these letters of their power!

LENCK How?

STEINDORFF You will announce to all that *you* are their author.

LENCK (*Beat.*) Me? Of . . . all those letters? But . . . how on earth is that possible?

STEINDORFF I don't know. Claim to be an adept calligraphist.

LENCK Ridiculous. And why would I do such a thing?

STEINDORFF Spin a heartbreaking tale regarding some callous lord of one city or the other who destroyed your family when you were a child.

LENCK And even if I succeed! I'll have evaded your father's anger and replaced it with the combined wrath of two armies girded for battle that would turn on *me* instead of on one another! But this post! This post, Herr Steindorff, is my opportunity to . . . to *fling off* the nursemaid's bonnet, yes, that is the mark of my low station, to show myself . . . to show *her* . . . (*Pause.*) You have no idea what it is like to be without what you have. But do not think it is deserved. It is nothing more than fortunate birth. So tell me, what man is less deserving of victory than the winner in a game of pure luck?

STEINDORFF The loser? (*Beat.*) I only mean: defeat will leave you without honor *and* with your debt intact. Does that prospect not frighten you more?

(*Pause.* LENCK *simply looks at* STEINDORFF.)

STEINDORFF So be it. I will summon soldiers in the morning to arrest you. And so I hope you have selected an audition piece with all its melodies clustered in the center of the keyboard.

LENCK Why is that?

STEINDORFF You will be able to reach little else. With your wrists shackled together.

(*Another bustle of entrance. The two men look up as a tide of cohorts once again disrupts the room.* SCHOTT, FASCH, *and* KAUFMANN *enter together.*)

KAUFMANN Gentlemen! Why do you keep us waiting?

SCHOTT (*Outraged, to* FASCH.) An alehouse fiddler! Speaking that way to me!

FASCH (*To* LENCK *and* STEINDORFF.) Please, won't you join us at last?

KAUFMANN We have encountered some lovely young women! But we require a third for dancing.

STEINDORFF (*Pointing to* SCHOTT.) You have a third.

FASCH Herr Schott will not dance.

SCHOTT I will not dance to *that*! A rondo, a bourrée, a passepied! What do the French know about dancing that the Germans do not?

FASCH Still, there was no need to become aggressive.

SCHOTT (*To* LENCK *and* STEINDORFF, *an appeal.*) I asked the tymbalist if he would plan an allemande. Or grace us with something by the masters of the last century: Tundert, Kerll, Hammerschmidt, Scheidt, Schein, Schütz.

STEINDORFF Gesundheit.

SCHOTT That was the man's reply exactly! And so I grabbed his neighbor's lute and smashed it on his chin.

(*Another exodus has begun. This time* KAUFMANN, SCHOTT, *and* STEINDORFF *go off together, with* FASCH *trailing a few steps behind.*)

KAUFMANN To the dance!

STEINDORFF Will Gisela not object to the spinning of tavern damsels?

KAUFMANN Oh, do you know her?

(KAUFMANN, STEINDORFF, *and* SCHOTT *are gone, this last fading.* FASCH *turns back to* LENCK, *who has remained still and silent throughout the hubbub.*)

FASCH Join us. We shall drink to an honorable competition in the morning.

LENCK Herr Fasch? May I have a . . . ?

FASCH What?

LENCK I do not know. For what I need there are, perhaps, no words.

(LENCK *begins to weep.*)

FASCH My dear Georg! What is the matter? What has so distressed you?

LENCK It is my Catherina. She has . . . taken ill.

FASCH Oh, I am sorry to hear it. (*Pause.*) Although I cannot say that I am surprised.

LENCK (*Perplexed.*) Oh? Why is that?

FASCH Well, I was never one to heed rumor particularly, but I have heard that a mysterious nursemaid called Bodenschatz attends her at the oddest hours of the—

LENCK Yes, well, one never knows when the worst of it may strike.

FASCH One never does. But what do you want of *me*?

LENCK Her treatment is most . . . expensive.

FASCH Ah.

LENCK Appallingly so. Why, to ensure her survival would cost some four hundred and thirty florins!

FASCH I say!

LENCK *And* eighteen groschen. And nine pfennig.

FASCH What sort of doctor would demand a king's ransom for survival itself?

LENCK It is not the fault of the doctor. He is expert in the use of all forms of emetics, sudorifics, febrifuges, and mercurials. But *this* illness is as rare as the lady herself. And there is only one cure. Which, by the way, will also require several horses and oxen.

FASCH Oxen? What sickness *is* this?

LENCK It is called . . . false pox.

FASCH (*Beat. He is not fooled.*) It sounds . . . harrowing.

LENCK It certainly is.

FASCH (*Playing along.*) And . . . her family will not help?

LENCK The Kirkendales despise me and are convinced that her illness is feigned, to steal their money!

FASCH (*Enjoying the game.*) Lenck, even if I had such an amount—and who does?—I am the wrong man to ask. Zerbst is in utter disarray.

LENCK Since when?

FASCH Why, since the flood!

LENCK Zerbst is in the mountains.

FASCH And thus we were most unprepared. Disease is rampant, and our doctors, never having learned to swim, all drowned. I have encountered every plague that nature has to offer on the roadside near my home. Indeed, I am surprised I have not encountered Catherina's false pox in my own township's fetid streets.

LENCK In a cruel twist of fate, it strikes only the extremely beautiful.

FASCH Then those closest to me are themselves at risk. My Anna has just borne us our first daughter, you see. They must both have every coin of mine at their disposal.

LENCK Think no more of it. You are a fine man.

FASCH I have no choice but to live humbly.

LENCK That is what I said.

FASCH I will pray, my friend, that her humors properly
  balance themselves.

(A moment. FASCH starts to laugh.)

LENCK Laughter, Fasch?
FASCH She is not sick at all, is she?
LENCK (Beat.) I cannot deceive you. For longer than I have
  already.
FASCH For what reason do you need money?
LENCK (A chuckle.) How long have you known me,
  Friedrich?
FASCH Since we tested the Liebfraukirche organ together in
  Sangerhausen, some . . . Oh, you mean how well do I
  know you. Oh, Lenck! What will happen if it is not
  repaid?
LENCK Arrest. Imprisonment. Worse, perhaps.
FASCH Then you must flee! Goodbye, Lenck.

(FASCH walks away.)

LENCK (Desperately.) My father, you know . . . was a
  wheelwright. Once, we resided on the land of a wealthy
  family. And one day we were banished, all of us.
FASCH What on earth are you—?
LENCK I watched as my mother died in penury, as my
  siblings scattered to alleyways and poorhouses, and I, the
  eldest, cared alone for my father, who, quite blind in his
  old age, would rave at me that I was not really his son.
  Then, one morning, his sight was restored! A tiny blessing
  at the end, I thought. Tiny indeed. That very day, he was
  felled by a massive seizure of the brain, the return of vision
  prefiguring only death. And no sooner had I left the home
  of the black-market surgeon to whom I sold his organs and

limbs than I vowed that all my loved ones would be avenged. But what power did I have to do so? I am a musician, yes. But I am also a gambler. And so I honed my skills. I even went so far as to seek the aid of my cousin, a mathematician. In fact, he lives in Zerbst. Perhaps you know him? Johann?

FASCH His name is also Johann?

LENCK No, his name is Maximilian. Why—?

FASCH Oh, I thought—

LENCK Ah. Yes. No. (*Beat.*) In any case, he is able to apply mathematics only to falling anchors and rolling boulders and such things, and was of no use.

FASCH (*Beat.*) What sort of mathematics does your cousin practice?

LENCK (*Very rapidly.*) Oh, he is a follower of Gottfried Leibniz, who has made it his business to unveil the numerical basis of the physical world, endeavoring to prove that a powerful order and meaning underlie even nature itself. (*Beat.*) Anyway, years later I returned to the site of my family's ruin, for a musical performance. Once there, I pursued an invitation to the evening card game hosted by the master of the house. Soon enough, I found myself seated across from the man himself. And, at stake, on our final hand, ownership of the very land where I was born.

FASCH And?

LENCK The trouble with cards, you see, is that even in a game of skill, in which queen, jester, and knave find meaning only in combination, the contest is reduced, at the last, to its simplest element. To luck alone.

FASCH What happened?

LENCK I turned mine. And he turned his. I had a pretty run of princes. But they were . . . insufficient, for he showed kings.

(LENCK *weeps again, this time in earnest.* FASCH *consoles him.*)

FASCH I wish that there was something I could do.

LENCK There is not. *(Pause.)* Unless—

FASCH Are you going to ask me to leave Leipzig?

LENCK Would you?

FASCH No.

LENCK But, Friedrich—

FASCH *No!* I have my own mission here, as you well know.

LENCK Then then let me help you! Yes! We can plot
together, to eliminate the others. Each must be vulnerable,
in, in *some* way—

FASCH Lenck, enough of this!

LENCK —to bribery or blackmail or, or *kidnapping*, and we'll
share the post, its honor, its *salary*, yes, I'll take on the
responsibilities you do not desire—

FASCH *Enough! (Pause.)* This post . . . this post, dear Lenck,
is my opportunity to rescue our musical future. But I will
have no mandate to do so if I seize it through thievery and
lies. Nor will I know, finally, in my heart, that I . . . that *he*
. . . *(Pause.)* A position with the power to guide music
must be gained *by* music! And music alone!

LENCK Do they have *politics* in Zerbst, Herr Fasch?

FASCH Periodically, yes. But the tactics you describe are
better suited to situations when ordinary principles are
suspended. To a state of a war.

LENCK Well, as they say, politics is only war by other means.
(Beat.) I only . . . You may find yourself with your
principles intact, watching the future of music from afar.
Does that prospect not frighten you more?

(*Pause.* FASCH *simply looks at* LENCK.)

LENCK So be it.

FASCH I am so sorry.

LENCK That is to be expected. I am pathetic. I am bathed in defeat as surely as summer is in heat!

FASCH Some summers are unseasonably cold.

LENCK Only to my personal disadvantage, I'm sure.

FASCH Oh, stop it! This is laziness disguised as despair. None of us control our condition at birth. To guide our lives thereafter is well within our means.

LENCK Oh? And what was *your* condition at birth, *Herr* Fasch? Nothing that stood in the way of your advancement, it seems. Nothing that prevented you from marrying the woman you love! Please. Not one of you would willingly trade lives with me now.

FASCH To believe that *anything* is inevitable is an abdication of your responsibility to live. You are a gambler, yes. But you are also a musician! Indeed, that is how I first remember you, at Sangerhausen, perched at the organ, eliciting from all its speaking stops the most delightful sounds. You have an honest chance here, Georg. We all do. Not least because . . . and I cannot be the only one who has noticed . . . *he* is not here. The Great—

LENCK Shh! Don't say his name! (*Beat.*) Superstition.

FASCH Very well. But his conspicuous absence is surely a providential sign!

LENCK But, Fasch, that is the worst of it. If not for all these years of poverty, of fleeing from debt and escaping from cold cells; if not for so many deaths of those I loved; if not for all the hardships thrust upon me by some unjust hand . . . Oh, Fasch! The music! The music I could write!

FASCH You still might! What is the alternative? To destroy the world as retaliation against its injustice?

LENCK Ah, well. (*Pause.*) In fact, Herr Fasch—

(*And a third time there is a bustle of entrance.* KAUFMANN, SCHOTT, *and* STEINDORFF *hurry into the room.* FASCH *is exasperated at the interruption.*)

FASCH Yes! Yes! We will join you in a moment!

KAUFMANN No, no! Help us! We need help!

(*For, it is now clear,* KAUFMANN *and* SCHOTT *are cradling* STEINDORFF, *who seems to have collapsed in their arms, barely able to walk, and who rambles vaguely as they convey him to a bench and lay him down.*)

STEINDORFF (*Slurred, confused.*) He will not . . . he will not let me . . .

FASCH What is this?

SCHOTT Betrayal! Skulduggery! By *your* hand!

FASCH I beg your pardon?

SCHOTT You shall not have it! For Steindorff has been drugged!

FASCH But . . . ! I . . . ! My vial is safely ensconced here in my cloak!

(KAUFMANN *raises a hand, holding up the vial for all to see: it is empty.*)

KAUFMANN We found this on the bench. Near Steindorff's goblet.

FASCH Someone must have taken it from me!

LENCK From your inside pocket? Ludicrous.

STEINDORFF He will not let me live!

SCHOTT Don't try to speak, Herr Steindorff. Guards! Guards!

FASCH Who, Martin? Who will not let you live?

STEINDORFF My father! (*Pause.*) I never wanted to be a musician. I wanted to be . . . a dancer! But he will not . . . he will not let me—!

(GRAUPNER *enters, arms raised triumphantly.*)

GRAUPNER Behold! Cower in fear! For standing now before
   you is the great—

(There is a pounding at the door of the church: three slow echoing crashes. The men look toward the sound. A shadow is cast across the floor by someone just out of view.)

GRAUPNER *(Beat.)* Damn.

(All bow toward the unseen man, except for SCHOTT, who turns out into a pool of light. The others follow in turn. And, during their letters, a man strides very slowly into view.)

SCHOTT

Leipzig. June, 1722.
   Herr Kuhnau:
      I write to you even though you are dead. For I am
   stunned to find myself surrounded by these men, these
   pretenders to your throne. And now . . .
GRAUPNER He's here. And, Doctor, now I see why they
   reserved for me the second largest room.
KAUFMANN Gisela, please send my scores as quickly as
   possible.
LENCK Catherina, please send more money as quickly as
   possible.
STEINDORFF I want to dance, Father! Why won't you let me
   dance?
FASCH Anna, a legend walks among us. And though I
   believe in it not, I feel as I did when you and I first met:
   that I am in the presence of destiny.

(The lights shift back. The new arrival is now downstage center, facing the double doors. He strides toward them, those in the

room parting before him like reeds and bowing as he passes.
He pulls open the doors. On this, SCHOTT *turns back out.)*

SCHOTT He has arrived. The Greatest Organist in Germany,
Georg Phillip Telemann, has arrived. You'll hear from me
again. In time.

Yours,

FASCH Johann.
LENCK Georg.
GRAUPNER Johann.
KAUFMANN Georg.
STEINDORFF Johann.
SCHOTT Georg.

(Six pigeons are released at once: wings . . . wind . . . a final
chord . . .)

(Blackout.)

Act Two

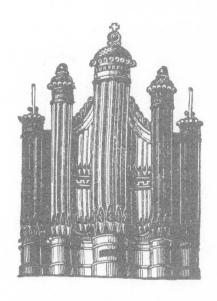

One

(FASCH, *alone.*)

FASCH

Leipzig. Late.

Anna:

Firstly, regarding your previous letter and the concerns you raised therein. I shall try, as you asked, to limit what you describe as the "all too numerous terms of endearment" I employ when addressing you in writing. If they do, as you say, "diminish" you, that was never my intent. As a musician, the only thing I wish to diminish is the occasional seventh. Also, I was astonished at your report that there has been a flood in Zerbst, which is, after all, in the mountains. Tell me, what has become of our home?

Speaking of which: you may be wondering about the moist condition of this paper. I write to you from the damp confines of a cell. I will not bore you with the details of my incarceration but, suffice it to say, I will require, as soon as you are able to send it, a new vial of the medicinal powder, which, I can assure you, is more effective than we ever imagined. I am working to secure my release in time for the audition, though, as a precaution, I have selected a piece whose melodies are clustered in the center of the keyboard.

I am thrilled at the news that you wish to try your hand at composition! I agree that our home need not fall silent simply because I am gone, and so I urge you to take up the mantle with vigor, you who have been my invisible support for so long! Thanks to you, our new daughter will hear music there even as I, here, attempt to provide her with a name. (*Pause.*) As to your question regarding what form your first attempt ought to take, you well know my opinion regarding the bounds of form: no less confining than the bars and walls of my current prison. I do concede, however, that it is difficult to begin anywhere else. After all, the styles of old must be understood thoroughly before they can be rejected as ridiculous. Innovation comes most easily when suppressed.

To that end, I recommend that you confront the dustiest form we have—cobwebs on its every surface, so limiting in its particulars that for every three notes there are twice that many rules to be obeyed. Yes, my will-o'-the-wisp . . . (*Beat.*) You, Anna, shall write a fugue. To begin, compose a melody played by a single voice.

(*Music begins: the Fugue in A Minor, for pipe organ, quietly, underneath.*)

This is called the *subject*. It must be beautiful enough to stand on its own, and well crafted enough to contain the potential for more. Indeed, as soon as it is finished . . . it is joined . . . by a Second Voice . . .

(*At this, the second voice enters in the music, and* SCHOTT *becomes visible. He is seated near the doors, as we first saw him. And, as* FASCH *continues to speak, and the music continues underneath,* SCHOTT *begins miming Act One, Scene Two, reenacting his repeated opening of the door, fluidly, like a dance. He mimes the scene as though* FASCH, *too, were retracing his steps, reacting to an absent interlocutor, though* FASCH, *for his part, simply continues with the letter to his wife.*)

. . . which begins its journey with its own statement of the subject, in a new octave, but reiterating, unmistakably, the theme. And, Anna, here is what distinguishes this form: your First Voice does not now descend into simple accompaniment. No! It plays a new theme, a *countersubject*. And as the First and Second Voices reach the end of this encounter . . . both are joined . . . by a Third Voice.

(At this, the third voice enters in the music, and LENCK *gradually becomes visible, both he and* SCHOTT *in place for the start of Act One, Scene Three, which they begin to mime, as above, behind* FASCH.*)*

Difficult task! For this must engage the subject, as the other two have done, even as the Second Voice embarks upon the countersubject. And the First? It moves on to realms uncharted. And all the while no voice is subordinate to the others. No voice is in command. No voice can content itself with echoing chords or oompah-pahs. On the contrary, the texture of the whole remains throughout a discussion among equals.

(Here the fugue reaches the cadence at the end of the third voice's development. FASCH *gives a gentle conductor's cutoff and the music fades.* LENCK *and* SCHOTT, *having reached the end of Act One, Scene Three, depart.)*

At this point, Anna, it might behoove you, as an amateur—a word I use descriptively, not in diminishment—to bring matters to a close. But you see now, I think, the further possibilities. How, in a process known as *fugal exposition*, a truly daring composer could here introduce . . .

(FASCH *gives the down beat with his hand and the music continues.* KAUFMANN *and* STEINDORFF *appear, miming through the top of Act One, Scenes Four and Five.*)

. . . a Fourth Voice . . . or a Fifth . . . each taking up the subject in its turn and in its way . . . each grappling with the countersubject as it comes . . . each introducing its own melodies and themes . . . and joining these to those that came before.

(LENCK *and* SCHOTT *return, miming the sequence of greetings. The music has now reached a section of episodic development.*)

Now, the subject need not be heard at all times. Indeed no, for then we'd be quite sick of it. On the contrary, the voices may seem, from time to time, to lose the subject altogether, engaging in what are called *episodes*, taking tangential turns and straying far afield, introducing ideas that seem entirely unrelated and wholly new. But they always return, sooner or later, to your theme.

(FASCH *points skyward and, at this, the subject does indeed reenter, high above, and the pantomime of this scene reaches the point of* SCHOTT's *impassioned speech.*)

And this, Anna, *this* is why it must be a most worthwhile melody: so that, bell-like, it will ring out each time it sounds.

(LENCK, SCHOTT, STEINDORFF, *and* KAUFMANN *exit.*)

To my knowledge, no composer has ever dared a fugue beyond Five Voices. But in theory one could, of course, hazard . . .

(GRAUPNER *appears, and mimes his letter from the top of Act One, Scene Six. During the following, he looks around and stalks off annoyed.*)

. . . a Sixth, sneaking in almost unnoticed, perhaps, given the complexity of that which has occurred already, but no less a distinct individual for being one in an increasing throng. And what then? How to proceed when all of your voices are deployed? What, then, indeed. For, now, the composer applies a series of what are called *fugal devices.*

(STEINDORFF *and then* SCHOTT *arrive for their clandestine meeting, and mime their scene.* FASCH, *for his part, is, in spite of himself, becoming more and more excited with this description.*)

When the theme reappears now, it is in a different mode altogether, its key signature shifted from minor to major . . . or it might be *augmented*, stretched so that it takes longer to unfold . . . or it might undergo *diminution*, passing with a quickened step.

(LENCK *and* KAUFMANN *enter from the tavern. After a brief flurry,* SCHOTT *and* KAUFMANN *exit, leaving* STEINDORFF *and* LENCK *behind to mime their scene.*)

The melody may now harmonize with itself, in *stretto*, or—and this is most difficult of all—be *inverted*, turned upside down, or run *backward*, if it is a crab canon, which can be read in any way at all, irrespective of direction!

(SCHOTT *and* KAUFMANN *return.* SCHOTT, STEINDORFF, *and* KAUFMANN *leave, while* LENCK *remains alone.*)

And these variations, Anna, give pleasure *only* in proportion to the attentiveness of the listener. For their significance derives, of course, from our knowledge of what has gone before. (FASCH *gestures, palms down, and the music fades.*) Then, a final riddle: how to end it? "The end of a fugue," Kuhnau once said to me, "must be surprising and yet inevitable. It must be both at once. All your voices must combine in miraculous polyphony, and that invisible lattice shall create a fabric of sound no single melody can ever achieve alone." What did he mean? you likely wonder.

(FASCH *gives the downbeat. The fugue reenters at a point near the climax.* FASCH *conducts as* KAUFMANN *and* SCHOTT *rush in, carrying* STEINDORFF, *miming accusations and ministrations.* GRAUPNER *appears. They all look toward the outside.* TELEMANN *appears. They bow to him. The men each turn out for their final letters.* TELEMANN *marches through them. And, as the triumphant last three chords ring out, he flings open the doors. The others turn out for their sign-offs and mime the release of their pigeons. We have reached the final tableau of the first act again.*)

What can follow next, save thunderous applause? (*The ghostly tableau fades away.* FASCH *is alone.*) If you like that sort of thing. I, as you know, care not for form. And do not feel badly, Anna, if you are mystified. Kuhnau's explanation did the same to me. It was not until I wrote a fugue myself that I understood, and, when I told him that the structure was now clear to me in retrospect, he remarked, "Structure is only clear in retrospect."

It grows late. And although this letter includes little about myself, I must ask you to copy over what you need, so that you might burn it, like the rest. I bridle at biography, as you know. Chapters? Where are those in my life? Those clear demarcations, sectioning time? Time does not chop itself up for our convenience. In a man's own life, time flows. It is always . . . now.

Yours, *Johann*

(*He releases a pigeon.*)

(*Blackout.*)

Two and Three and Four and Five

(The anteroom. LENCK *and* GRAUPNER, *sitting. A moment.)*

LENCK They've kept us waiting for some time, don't you
  think?

GRAUPNER In what sense?

LENCK In the sense that we began waiting quite some time
  ago and the waiting period has yet to conclude.

*(*KAUFMANN *enters.)*

KAUFMANN Good morning!

GRAUPNER Hello, Herr Kaufmann.

KAUFMANN Am I too late?

LENCK Your audition is not until much later today. I'm first.
  Graupner is second.

GRAUPNER Naturally.

LENCK The order is posted in a vestibule, behind one of the
  chapels.

KAUFMANN So I'm told. I am, however, having difficulty
  finding it. Which chapel?

GRAUPNER The seventh from the left. But each is divided
  into three sections, which are, of course, sectioned into
  various divisions.

LENCK Hope that helps.

KAUFMANN *(Moving to exit.)* As do I.

LENCK I think you may be last of the seven.

KAUFMANN Eight.

GRAUPNER What?

KAUFMANN An eighth candidate arrived this morning. From Cöthen. Perhaps you know him? Johann?

GRAUPNER Which Johann?

KAUFMANN No, I was asking if you, Johann, know him.

LENCK (*Thinking he understands.*) His name is *not* Johann.

KAUFMANN In fact, it is. Johann Bach. He delayed his journey due to the birth of a son. Not his first, to be sure, but an event nevertheless.

LENCK How is Steindorff this morning?

KAUFMANN Gone, I'm afraid.

LENCK *Dead?*

KAUFMANN No, merely gone. They found his room empty. No one had seen him leave.

LENCK And did you happen to notice any . . . soldiers in the streets this morning?

KAUFMANN Soldiers? No. But then I have not ventured beyond the borders of the Thomaskirchof since I heard tell of that unearthly moaning footpad, hooded and ragged, stalking the roads . . . Terrifying! (*He shudders.*) Seventh from the left, you said?

GRAUP⎫
LENCK ⎬ Right.

KAUFMANN Oh, dear.

(KAUFMANN *goes.*)

LENCK I'm relieved to hear that Steindorff is, at the very least, ambulatory.

GRAUPNER As am I. To come upon such a scene!

LENCK Oh, I'm sure. But I'm afraid that I must bear some of the responsibility for the presence of the powder in his beer.

GRAUPNER How so?

LENCK I put it there.

GRAUPNER Really! But why?

LENCK With the vial so accessible, right there, tucked into the lining of Fasch's inside shirt pocket, just barely beneath his jacket, I was tempted. To improve my chances.

GRAUPNER But Fasch has been imprisoned for the crime!

LENCK And thus it was more effective than I ever intended. Am I awful?

GRAUPNER You are . . . only human. I witness the desire to silence the competition each time I look inside myself.

LENCK In fact . . . with Telemann here . . . one might argue that the call for extreme measures is that much starker. That drugging Steindorff represents only one possible such measure among many. And that, now, to focus on one another is a waste of effort *better* spent swaying the Council itself.

GRAUPNER One might. If one were so inclined.

LENCK After all, any gambler knows that you'll seldom find friendlier odds . . . than one in two.

GRAUPNER (*Pause.*) What are you proposing, Lenck?

LENCK I have proposed nothing. Why? Are you open to a proposal of some kind?

GRAUPNER That depends, naturally, upon what is being proposed.

LENCK We can agree, I think, that, in the presence of a legend, this day will no longer be decided by the sounds we each produce from the instrument.

GRAUPNER Well! When the Council hears my audition—

LENCK Ah, but that is the trouble. However sweet the bellows you produce from the organ pipes, they will be no match for the sound of a name all Germany will recognize!

GRAUPNER I . . . suppose . . .

LENCK Fortunately, there is *another* sound that sways men more profoundly still.

GRAUPNER Out with it, Lenck.

LENCK A jingle, Herr Graupner.

GRAUPNER You intend to *buy* the post? Just as the Catholics bought indulgences?

LENCK No. Not *just* as the Catholics bought indulgences. For one thing, I intend to buy the post in secret.

GRAUPNER Martin Luther did not nail his ninety-five theses to the great doors at Wittenberg only to have *you* seize the most coveted post in German music using your wealth!

LENCK You mistake my meaning.

GRAUPNER Oh? Then I apologize.

LENCK I had hoped to use *your* wealth.

GRAUPNER *What?*

LENCK Not for my benefit alone! I am prepared to *share* the post with an accomplice. And so I thought to myself, Who here draws the largest salary? But of course Telemann has no use for me, so then I thought, Who here draws the second largest?

GRAUPNER *(Quietly.)* "Don't while away your worth worrying if you're worthwhile."

LENCK What?

GRAUPNER Georg, even if I had such an amount—and I do—how much of my fortune do you think I carry with me when I travel?

LENCK No matter! With my skill at the card table, I can produce the requisite sum. *You* must simply provide me with an initial stake that exceeds my current means. And then I will content myself with whatever responsibilities you do not desire. Presiding over the Thomasschule, say, while you bask in the glory of composition and performance.

GRAUPNER I hesitate to rely so much on the chance turn of a card.

LENCK There is no chance involved! My cousin is a mathematician, a follower of Leibniz, and has provided me with ironclad methods for victory!

GRAUPNER How does the behavior of flags in wind apply to gambling?

LENCK *(Beat.)* You are familiar with Leibniz.

GRAUPNER I am a great admirer of his. Indeed, in a practice I learned from my old teacher, I have my favorite Leibnizian sayings nailed to the walls of my study. Above my washbasin it says "Music is nothing but unconscious arithmetic." I prefer to rely on certainties, Georg. Not luck. My devotion to Calvinism allows me to accept nothing less.

LENCK *(Beat.)* You are a Calvinist, Herr Graupner?

GRAUPNER Yes. In Darmstadt they call it Graupnerism.

LENCK Really?

GRAUPNER *(Small pause.)* No.

LENCK But you have heard of the animosity between Merseburg and Zwickau?

GRAUPNER Of course! Merseburg is respectful of its Calvinist citizens, whereas in Zwickau they are cruelly persecuted.

LENCK Intolerance is purely the result of irrational fear.

GRAUPNER Indeed. They must be crushed so that Calvinism can rule all Germany.

LENCK Yes. *(Beat.)* And so I can confess to you, and you alone, the truth. Just now . . . when I asked after Steindorff's well-being . . . it was only to determine whether or not he had been . . . *found.*

GRAUPNER Found?

LENCK Even now, Zwickau's prodigal son lies bound and gagged in the forest outside the gates! In his stupor, I kidnapped him and put him there!

GRAUPNER But . . . why?

LENCK *(Ethereally, wonderstruck.)* I felt I had no choice. As though guided by some invisible hand toward supporting the Calvinist cause.

GRAUPNER That, Herr Lenck, was divine will!

LENCK *(Reverently.)* I don't doubt it. And it was that same force that seemed to demand that I approach you with this plan. Might it be that, together, we are God's allies, and that any joint endeavor is *certain* to succeed?

GRAUPNER It just might.

LENCK So are you with me? Or is it true what they say?

GRAUPNER What's that?

LENCK That you are only the second most daring organist in Germany.

(*The double doors swing open.* LENCK *slowly walks toward them.*)

GRAUPNER Wait! (*Pause.*) I cannot deny it. I spent the morning cursing Telemann's very presence, for making mine completely moot. Indeed, if not for all the patronage denied me and handed to him . . . Oh, Lenck! The music! The music I could write!

LENCK Well said.

GRAUPNER And this post . . . this post, Lenck, is my opportunity to prove myself the superior musician!

LENCK Plied with enough coins, the Council will be forced to admit it at last!

GRAUPNER I'll leave the money in your room.

(*They shake hands.* KAUFMANN *enters, unseen.*)

LENCK Splendid, Herr Graupner. If there is one man in all Germany upon whom you can rely to scheme until this post is yours, and also somewhat mine, well, sir, that man is—
    Herr Kaufmann, how unexpectedly you've returned!

KAUFMANN I failed once again to find the list. What's going on?

GRAUPNER Herr Lenck . . . and I . . . are . . .

LENCK Rehearsing. A dramatic reading we shall perform for the rest of you.

KAUFMANN Oh, really? When?

LENCK This very evening. At eight o'clock exactly. Employing this . . . strikingly theatrical room itself as our set.

KAUFMANN Is it a comedy?

LENCK Oh, yes.

KAUFMANN What is it called?

LENCK *The Unbelievably Credulous Fool.*

KAUFMANN It sounds hilarious!

LENCK It is. (*Beat.*) Excuse me. (*He turns toward the doors.*)

GRAUPNER Do you have your music?

LENCK Oh. Yes.

(LENCK *opens his coat, revealing scores, strapped to his torso. He frees them, smooths them, and exits through the doors, which close behind him.*)

KAUFMANN A play! How delightful! I have been a devotee of the theatre ever since my mother took me to Paris as a child. We took in the latest by Molière at his Illustre Theatre. I was transported.

GRAUPNER Were you?

KAUFMANN Yes. Hundreds of miles. I fell asleep inside a crate of props. When I awoke, I was in Turkey.

(SCHOTT *enters.*)

SCHOTT Kaufmann, what are you doing here? Your audition is not until—

KAUFMANN Yes, much later today. But I cannot find the list.

SCHOTT Vestibule. Seventh from the left.

KAUFMANN Ah! (*He turns to go.*)

SCHOTT How is Steindorff this morning? Dead?

KAUFMANN (*Turning back.*) No. Vanished. Left, you said?

SCHOTT You said he left. I was the one who asked.

KAUFMANN What? *(Beat.)* Oh, dear.

(KAUFMANN goes.)

GRAUPNER So. One of our own, gone.

SCHOTT Yes, but the number of candidates holds steady. Another has arrived—

GRAUPNER From Cöthen, yes—

SCHOTT Apparently, he delayed his journey pending the birth of two or three sons.

GRAUPNER Yes. *(Beat.)* Still, it is a shame. Steindorff, lost . . .

SCHOTT And I must confess that, in the matter of his drugging, the fault lies more or less with me.

GRAUPNER In . . . what way?

SCHOTT I drugged him.

GRAUPNER You were tempted to improve your chances. With the vial so accessible—

SCHOTT Right there, on the bench, next to the goblet Lenck had prepared especially for Steindorff—

GRAUPNER And Fasch has been imprisoned for the crime.

SCHOTT Exactly as I intended.

GRAUPNER And yet . . . with Telemann here . . . one must allow that the odds are not yet . . . ideal.

SCHOTT *(Beat.)* What are you suggesting?

GRAUPNER You overestimate my subtlety. I have not suggested it yet. *(Pause.)* It's true, is it not, that Kuhnau never named a preferred successor?

SCHOTT No one, I think, was more surprised by Kuhnau's death than Kuhnau.

GRAUPNER And would knowledge of his wishes tip the balance here?

SCHOTT We may bid the dead to speak, but they cannot.

GRAUPNER Oh, but they can.

(With a flourish, GRAUPNER *produces a document from inside his cloak.)*

SCHOTT What's that?

GRAUPNER A letter. Or, no, not a letter but a piece of music that, when decoded, contains a message. From Johann Kuhnau. I received it shortly before he died. Shall I translate it for you?

SCHOTT I expect that you shall.

GRAUPNER

"Leipzig. May, 1722.

"My dear Johann:

"I am not as strong as I once was. Daily, I can feel shadowy tendrils encroaching upon the edges of my vision. It will be time, presently, for someone to take my place here. If possible, I hope to secure for myself a role in the decision, if need be from beyond the grave. To that end, please come to see me at once. Godspeed, my friend. I look forward to seeing you soon.

"Yours, *Johann*"

SCHOTT He takes quite some time to say very little.

GRAUPNER Yes, he was well known for his long and elaborate missives.

SCHOTT Perhaps. But you were not able to speak to him as he asked?

GRAUPNER The letter reached me too late. A peasant shot down and ate the pigeon bearing it.

SCHOTT So you cannot be sure of what he meant.

GRAUPNER I think the implication is clear.

SCHOTT Someone attempting to be clear needn't bother with implication.

GRAUPNER Oh, but its vagueness speaks to its authenticity. If I'd written it myself, would I not have been as explicit as possible?

SCHOTT Certainly. But you are left without decisive

backing: the Council will not be persuaded simply because you give them your word.

GRAUPNER You mistake my meaning.

SCHOTT *(Beat.)* Had you hoped to use *my* word?

GRAUPNER Not for my benefit alone! It's true, is it not, that, as a child, despite numerous applications, you were never admitted to the Thomasschule?

SCHOTT No! No, I *chose* to . . . to learn from my . . . How do you know that?

GRAUPNER Kuhnau was my teacher, and I his most cherished pupil. He told me of your rejection, after rejection, after rejection—

SCHOTT His standards were most unjust! Valuing wealth and status above talent!

GRAUPNER Nonsense. He admitted many who were needy.

SCHOTT So you say.

GRAUPNER It is well documented. He financed entire educations from his own pocket.

SCHOTT Very well—

GRAUPNER There is a famous story of an orphan boy he found starving in an alley—

SCHOTT Enough!

GRAUPNER Took him in, raised him as his only son—

SCHOTT Get to the point!

GRAUPNER While *you* clawed your way to a post at the Neuekirche, the second most important position in Leipzig! And, believe me, it's an indignity I well know. You became colleagues. Peers! You devoted all your energies to this pursuit, never remarrying, never having children, and now an *audition*! The very fact of it must enrage you.

SCHOTT *Yes!* *(Beat.)* So, for what reason in this life would I secure your victory?

GRAUPNER None in this life, perhaps. But think ahead. To your own posterity. When chosen, I will be in a position to reward you. I can place you in charge of the Thomasschule, the very institution that denied you so persistently. While I undertake the arduous work of composition and performance, I would place in your hands, Balthasar, the responsibility for shaping our next generation of musicians.

(*The double doors open.* LENCK *emerges.*)

LENCK They're ready for you, Graupner. Hello, Schott. Best of luck to you both.

(LENCK *exits, with a glance at* GRAUPNER. *A moment.*)

GRAUPNER Lenck, by the way, intends to bribe his way into the post.
SCHOTT You don't say.
GRAUPNER I just have. He has offered to ally himself with me. But he is worse than Pietist, Balthasar. He is godless. Bound by nothing at all. I value freedom, but freedom must have limits. And I see in *you* a kindred spirit! One who likewise recognizes the threat to our faith—
SCHOTT Sprouting from within.
GRAUPNER Yes! So are you with me? Or do you prefer to risk rejection once again?
SCHOTT Wait! (*Pause.*) I confess, if not for my banishment to a secondary post without influence or honor; if not for being denied access to my own city's resident master while every destitute half-wit between here and the Caucasus steeped themselves in his knowledge; if not for the irreparable loss, the unfilled void of my . . . of my . . . Oh, Graupner!
GRAUPNER The music! The music you could write!
SCHOTT And this post would render all my sacrifices worthwhile! It is my chance to demonstrate that I

am equipped not simply to study there but to
rule!

GRAUPNER After I have unilaterally granted you the
position, the Council will have no choice but to
acknowledge your qualifications.

SCHOTT Good Christoph. Please accept my aid.

(KAUFMANN *enters, unseen.*)

GRAUPNER Excellent. When the others are defeated, we will
rule the musical world, and echoing from hilltop to
riverbed shall be the glorious names—
   Kaufmann! You've somehow learned to materialize from
nowhere!

KAUFMANN Have I? I had no idea.

GRAUPNER Well. Excuse me.

SCHOTT Do you have your music?

GRAUPNER Oh. Yes.

(GRAUPNER *reaches into his trousers, carefully unties the thread,
produces a few scores, smooths them, and exits through the doors,
which close behind him.*)

KAUFMANN That speech was marvelously performed, don't
you think?

SCHOTT What?

KAUFMANN Are you going to be in the dramatic reading as
well?

SCHOTT (*Pause.*) What?

(FASCH *enters, massaging his wrists.*)

KAUFMANN Fasch!

FASCH Kaufmann, what are you doing here? Your audition is
not until—

KAUFMANN Yes, I know, but I found the proper vestibule
and the list is not there!

FASCH They moved it. The previous location, they
determined, was too difficult to find. *(Beat.)* How is
Steindorff this morning?

KAUFMANN Enough! Why are you all hounding me? I didn't
mean to drug him!

FASCH *You?*

KAUFMANN Well, I saw Herr Schott doing it, and Herr
Lenck doing it, and I thought perhaps Herr Steindorff was
having trouble sleeping, and so I tried to help! I am sorry!
Now leave me alone.

(KAUFMANN exits. A moment.)

SCHOTT You have been released, I see.

FASCH And I see that none of you were willing to help,
despite your guilt.

SCHOTT *Because* of our guilt, Fasch. To exchange your
disadvantage for ours would be foolish. *(Pause.)* For . . .
with Telemann here . . . the odds—

FASCH Herr Schott. Are you going to formulate a nefarious
plan, with me as your accomplice, whereby the number of
candidates can be reduced to two?

SCHOTT Would you be amenable to such a formulation?

FASCH Certainly not.

SCHOTT Excellent, as I have no such plan. *(Pause.)* How did
you secure your release, by the way?

FASCH I showed the guards . . . *this.*

*(FASCH produces a metal case from his coat and opens it,
removing a letter.)*

SCHOTT *(Alarmed.)* What's that?

FASCH It's a letter. Or, no, not a letter—

SCHOTT But a melody that when decoded contains a
   message?
FASCH Yes. Which—
SCHOTT You received from Kuhnau shortly before he died?
FASCH Why, *yes*. And in it—
SCHOTT There is a clear implication that Kuhnau wished for
   you to succeed him?
FASCH How on earth did you know?
SCHOTT I expect that now you shall translate it for me.
FASCH Very well, I shall!

> "Leipzig. May, 1722.
>
> "My dear Johann:
>   "I'm dying, and I wish to choose a replacement. Come
> at once.
>
> "Yours, *Johann*"

SCHOTT He says so much with so little.
FASCH Yes, he was widely known for the concision and
   brevity of his letters.
SCHOTT Perhaps. (*Pause.*) But you were not able to speak to
   him as he asked.
FASCH (*Beat.*) You physically barred the door!
SCHOTT Oh, yes, that's right. (*Beat.*) I only mean that, in
   your letter, nothing explicit is said.
FASCH Well, yes. But does that not—
SCHOTT In some way speak to its authenticity? I suppose.
FASCH Though it does leave me—
SCHOTT Without decisive backing.
FASCH Yes.
SCHOTT And no one will be persuaded simply because you
   give them your word.
FASCH (*Beat.*) Are you offering to vouch for my letter, Herr
   Schott?
SCHOTT You underestimate my alacrity. I have offered
   already.

FASCH But . . . for what reason in this life would you—?

SCHOTT None. But think ahead. To my own posterity.

FASCH (*Beat.*) What?

SCHOTT In exchange, you would give me authority over the Thomasschule.

FASCH You? In charge of the students?

SCHOTT Is that so preposterous?

FASCH The school never admitted you to begin with!

SCHOTT *How does everyone know that?*

FASCH He *rejected* you, again, and again, and again, and—

SCHOTT His criteria were horribly narrow!

FASCH He once admitted a boy with no hands.

SCHOTT All right!

FASCH Not much of a virtuoso, but quite musical, he would—

(SCHOTT *grabs the hilt of his sword and draws a portion of the blade.*)

SCHOTT Careful, Fasch.

FASCH What sort of man comes to an audition armed?

SCHOTT Pragmatic men travel everywhere armed, in a world where marauders seem to own the roads outside the city. And usurpers own them within.

FASCH Are you threatening *violence?*

SCHOTT Not. Yet. But where reason fails, more direct methods become necessary.

FASCH In that case, why not simply destroy the organ? The new Thomaskantor would be without an instrument, and the prominence of your post at the Neuekirche would rise to fill the void. (*Beat.*) That was a joke.

SCHOTT Of course.

(*The double doors open.* GRAUPNER *emerges.* SCHOTT *hides his sword.*)

GRAUPNER They're ready for you, Herr Schott. Fasch. *(Beat.)* Best of luck.

(GRAUPNER *exits, with a glance at* SCHOTT. *A moment.*)

SCHOTT Graupner, by the way, also intends to invoke Kuhnau's wishes.

FASCH On what grounds?

SCHOTT He also has a letter. And has offered to ally himself with me. But I see in you a kindred spirit!

FASCH No you don't.

SCHOTT Perhaps not. But he is worse than Pietist! He is choiceless! Bound by everything! I value limits, but even limits must have . . . limits! Do not surrender Leipzig to the Calvinists. Your letter will hold no sway without my help. You would do well to ask for it while it is still being offered.

(SCHOTT *walks slowly toward the double doors. He stops. He looks back at Fasch.*)

FASCH Oh, um, good luck.

SCHOTT Aren't you going to ask me to wait?

FASCH What for?

SCHOTT Because! My movement toward the door indicates that the opportunity to form a partnership is slipping away!

FASCH But our beliefs are completely irreconcilable!

SCHOTT And will the Council's decision adhere to your principles or to mine?

FASCH Their failure of vision must not cause our own. That is what having principles means. Indeed, while you claim to believe that there are no accidents, your behavior now suggests the opposite: that you think you will have nothing that you do not seize by force.

SCHOTT I might say the same to you.

FASCH You might, but it would be strange.

SCHOTT No, Friedrich. While you claim to guide your destiny, in fact you even now allow the gates of heaven to open at the capricious behest of an unseen hand. *(He gestures to the doors.)* Seize the handle yourself. Now!

FASCH No.

(KAUFMANN enters, unseen.)

SCHOTT Very well! But I swear that I will *take* the honor that has been so long denied me. And if you stand in my way I shall not only show you my weapon but draw it, and carve into your very flesh, as an eternal reminder of your folly, the name—

Kaufmann! Damn you, you stealthy dog!

KAUFMANN I must say, this appears to be the most thrilling play imaginable!

SCHOTT ⎫
FASCH ⎭ *(Beat.)* What?

KAUFMANN Please, stop your rehearsal. I want to see it all for the first time, with fresh eyes, able to anticipate none of the surprises in store for me.

SCHOTT I'm sure you are safe in that, Herr Kaufmann. *(Pause.)* Excuse me.

(SCHOTT goes to the double doors.)

FASCH Do you have your music?

SCHOTT Oh. Yes.

(SCHOTT reaches into his mouth and removes a tightly folded score from beneath his tongue. He unfolds it and exits through the double doors, which close behind him.)

FASCH A *play*, did you say?

KAUFMANN Yes! The one to be performed tonight! I think, perhaps, if I like it, I will bring it home to Merseburg.

FASCH I saw Molière performed at his Illustre Theatre in Paris once. I hated it. I chafed under the artifice. It depicted a world in which we are as bestringed as any cello and thus banished . . . *meaning*. The characters all happened to disagree about whatever was centrally at stake; every action was designed to further events; people always entered at exactly the proper moment. . . . The Creator's hand was all too clear.

KAUFMANN What is the alternative?

FASCH To write a play in which the demands of its form do not supersede the truthfulness of its content! To stop hiding what we are behind tired conventions: the deus ex machina; or the messenger who arrives with insanely detailed knowledge of tremendous events approaching from a distance; or, or, the fool who suddenly speaks wisdom—

KAUFMANN But . . . forgive me, Fasch . . . what's the difference?

FASCH Between . . . ?

KAUFMANN Between the form and the content? Rather . . . how is it possible to write . . . formlessly? What is the difference, finally, between choices that lead to a destiny and a destiny prefigured by certain choices? Let's say *you* are the Creator. And you wish to give your characters choice. As you write, the choices are *yours*. As the play is performed, the choices are *theirs*. Your audience is aware of both, so both are true. And, it seems to me, you cannot deny one without denying the other. Where those onstage have control, so do you. Where you have none, neither do they. After all, if you seat your characters in an unchanging place, at the mercy of some unseen force, conversing to no purpose, passing time . . . Well, there is no destiny in that world, to be sure, but no choice, either. And even *that* is a form. A formless form. Ha-ha. This old world, Fasch, will be new again, and again, and so after us will come new forms we cannot imagine, because we do not yet need them to explain the world to ourselves. Which is, in the end, all they are meant for: not to hide what we are. But to remind us.

FASCH *(Pause.)* Yes. *(Pause.)* Well. *(Pause.)* I still hate Molière.

KAUFMANN The discipline remains unperfected. That is why there are still playwrights. *(Beat.)* And now I must go off again in search of that list. Where did you say they had moved it?

FASCH I didn't.

KAUFMANN Ah, that may be the source of my confusion.

(KAUFMANN *turns and goes before* FASCH *can speak again. The doors open and* SCHOTT *emerges, pale and shaken.*)

FASCH Herr Schott! Why are you finished so quickly?

SCHOTT I was interrupted. The Council cut me off in mid-phrase.

FASCH But why?

SCHOTT They have grown impatient and decided to change the order.

FASCH But then . . . Who is next?

(TELEMANN *appears. A moment. Then he walks toward the doors, music tucked under one arm, ignoring the bows from the other two as he passes between them. He opens the doors, flexes his fingers once, and exits.* FASCH *and* SCHOTT *close the doors behind him.*)

SCHOTT I really hate him. *(Pause.)* Well! If the Council
imagines that I shall sit here, waiting, they are mistaken.
For I shall not.

FASCH Yes. Yes. Nor I.

SCHOTT Well, then. *(Pause.)* I'll be off. *(Pause.)* Best to you
and yours, Johann.

FASCH And yours, Georg.

(Blackout.)

Six

(*The anteroom, hours later.* FASCH *and* SCHOTT *are seated outside the double doors.*)

SCHOTT It's been a long while since he went inside, don't you think?

FASCH In what sense?

SCHOTT In the sense that he went inside a long while ago and has not yet emerged.

FASCH It's nearly eight o'clock. You're quite right. (*Pause.*) Herr Schott.

SCHOTT What.

FASCH Do you want to know *why* Kuhnau rejected you from the Thomasschule?

SCHOTT What? Well, I . . . (*Beat.*) Did he *tell* you?

FASCH Yes.

SCHOTT I . . . (*Pause.*) What did he say?

FASCH That you were in one sense a brilliant young musician. That your compositions were exquisitely well crafted. Each note in place. Every rule obeyed. But that in another sense you were not a musician at all. That the ineffable beauty that transcends structure eluded you. Never an original melody. No note a surprise. He felt, Balthasar, that he had nothing to teach you. And that the things you lacked could not be taught.

SCHOTT (*Pause.*) Why are you telling me these things?

FASCH Because despite them, or perhaps even because of them, I—

(KAUFMANN *hurries in, excitedly.*)

KAUFMANN Am I too late?

FASCH For your audition?

KAUFMANN No! I was told that tonight, in this very room, at this very hour, I could witness the world-premiere performance of an hilarious new comedy entitled *The Unbelievably Credulous Fool.* But, Fasch, I did take your comments very much to heart. So I intend to observe with the eye of a craftsman not easily taken in by artifice. So, please! Begin!

(KAUFMANN *seats himself and watches expectantly. A moment.*)

FASCH What was I talking about?

KAUFMANN Ah, *in medias res.* The classic opening.

FASCH It is possible that they are offering him the post at this very moment.

SCHOTT Kuhnau's post *is* the Council's to fill.

KAUFMANN My word! This script is remarkably apropos.

FASCH
SCHOTT } Shut up, Kaufmann.

KAUFMANN And highly experimental as well.

FASCH And so I accept your offer. Let us combine our efforts. I will take the kirche, you the schule.

KAUFMANN Oho! The plot thickens.

FASCH (*Offering his hand.*) Are we agreed?

SCHOTT (*Pause. He accepts the handshake.*) Yes.

(*With a swirl of his cloak,* TELEMANN *enters. Not from the double doors but from the direction of the rooms. He is dressed for travel, as he was when he arrived.* KAUFMANN, *seeing him, gasps. A moment. Then he crosses, not glancing at* FASCH *and* SCHOTT, *who bow, and exits to the outside.*)

KAUFMANN Oh, cleverly done! For I assumed that it *was* Telemann in the room with the Council! Now, a vacuum of knowledge has been created, begging the question: why is Herr Telemann departing?

FASCH (*To* KAUFMANN.) Herr Telemann was offered the post this afternoon, but he has turned it down. It seems he negotiated in advance, with his employers at Hamburg, securing a promise that they would triple his salary to keep him. (*Beat.*) He has, by the way, a gorgeous speaking voice.

KAUFMANN Direct address to the audience is by far the laziest form of exposition.

FASCH (*Beat.*) *What?*

KAUFMANN And we now also wonder: who is inside, after all?

(*The double doors open.* GRAUPNER *emerges.* KAUFMANN *gasps again.*)

SCHOTT What has happened?

FASCH What did they say?

GRAUPNER They've offered me the post.

(KAUFMANN *gasps most loudly of all. A beat.*)

SCHOTT And I look forward to sharing it with you, as you promised.

FASCH No, Balthasar!

GRAUPNER That promise was made in return for support you did not give me. And which proved unnecessary, in any case.

SCHOTT But you nevertheless feel loyal to my intent.

FASCH And what of *Kuhnau's* intent? Made clear in his letter to me?

GRAUPNER You also have a letter?

FASCH Yes.

GRAUPNER $\Big\}$ But *mine* is genuine.
FASCH

SCHOTT Fasch's letter is a forgery! I vouch for Herr Graupner!

GRAUPNER Schott, the point is moot. In fact—

(Suddenly, with a howl, LENCK *sprints in. He is wearing only rags, and waving a sword.* KAUFMANN *leaps up, as* LENCK *collapses in the center of the room, wailing.)*

KAUFMANN Run! It's the demented thief from the woods!

SCHOTT It's Lenck.

GRAUPNER Yes, the man from the woods had a hood concealing his face.

KAUFMANN Oh, thank goodness. Spectacular entrance, Lenck!

GRAUPNER Where have you been?

LENCK At the tavern.

GRAUPNER Ah. *(Beat. He looks* LENCK *over.)* And how did that work out for you?

LENCK Not well. I've lost everything.

FASCH $\Big\}$ All the money I gave you?
GRAUPNER

FASCH This is becoming ridiculous.

GRAUPNER *(To* LENCK.*)* So much for your intent to bribe the Council.

FASCH *(Baffled.)* Bribe the Council?

GRAUPNER *(Earnestly confused.)* Oh, were you not a part of that particular scheme?

FASCH Certainly not! And I know better than to hand coins to Lenck himself. No, he sent an emissary, a loyal nursemaid called Bodenschatz. She assured me that Lenck was quite ill with a severe case of something called the swindles! *(Beat.)* Oh, I see.

LENCK Then, with the money gone, I lost Schott's necklace.

SCHOTT I knew it!

FASCH And your clothing was the last to go.

LENCK Oh, how I wish. But finally, you see, determined to win it all back, I reached into my shirt, cut the straps, and bet my music. And . . . Even when I'd lost my scores—all of them—I thought, surely, the man would give them back. What possible use for them could this, this tavern keeper, have?

But he smiled! "Don't worry, little musician, I have found a use for them, after all. This summer, you see, is unseasonably cold." And it was then that I noticed that, despite wearing only these rags, I was . . . I was quite . . . *warm*. A vibrant fire raged across the room. And I? I ran.

(*A moment.* KAUFMANN *clutches his chest, moved by the speech.*)

KAUFMANN Bravo! Bravo! Oh, it is a masterful comedy that can be moving as well!

LENCK Thank you, Kaufmann. But I would never have written such a role for myself had I the choice.

SCHOTT Are you the one who has him so confused?

LENCK As you know, Herr Schott, I found him that way.

FASCH Georg, I am . . . so sorry.

LENCK No need! For, on my way across the courtyard, whom should I encounter but Herr Telemann, departing! And on his lips the latest news! Is it true, Christoph? Are you the second choice for the post?

GRAUPNER I . . . did Telemann use those words?

LENCK Yes. He has, by the way, a gorgeous speaking voice.

GRAUPNER It's true.

LENCK And I look forward to sharing it with you, as you promised!

SCHOTT No, Christoph!

GRAUPNER But all you did was lose my money! You failed
utterly to bribe anyone! And the scheme was unnecessary,
in any case!

LENCK Yes, but given my noble intent—

GRAUPNER Lenck, the point is moot! In fact—

(STEINDORFF *enters, in rags, limping, stumbling, festooned with
leaves and branches, howling. A hood conceals his face and his
hands are bound. Indeed, for this reason his identity is not
immediately clear.* KAUFMANN *leaps up.*)

KAUFMANN Run! It is the Ghostly Footpad of the Forest!
Hooded, as you said!

LENCK No, it's only Steindorff.

STEINDORFF Kaufmann! Free my hands! Uncover my head!

KAUFMANN Audience participation! Revolutionary!

(KAUFMANN *frees* STEINDORFF.)

STEINDORFF Who has done this to me?

FASCH In fact, Martin, the question of who drugged your
beer is a complex one.

STEINDORFF What? No. *That* I did myself. I mean, how
often does one have the chance to sample high-quality
opium?

FASCH It is not opium!

STEINDORFF Fasch, I think I know opium when I ingest it.

FASCH No! It is . . . a mysterious powder from . . . the Far
East . . . with the power to ease pain and bring about . . .
pleasant dreams . . . oh, dear . . .

STEINDORFF But then as I lay in my drugged state a crime
took place. I was kidnapped! Taken deep into the forest
and dropped there! I traveled, blind! I was robbed by
peasants, who stole my boots, which contained my music!
All day passed with no sustenance, and I became so

hungry that I was forced to kill and eat a messenger pigeon. But I forged onward. And, happy day, I enter at exactly the proper moment to find all the potential culprits gathered together!

KAUFMANN I see your point, Fasch. It does smack of contrivance.

FASCH It's over, Steindorff. Herr Graupner has been offered the post.

STEINDORFF Graupner? *(Beat.)* I think I've heard the name, but I'm not quite—

GRAUPNER Gentlemen! The point is moot! In fact—

KAUFMANN No, no, no! It would be much funnier if, at this point, Graupner were interrupted for a *third* time. Please consider making that revision. *(Beat.)* Carry on.

GRAUPNER I've rejected the post! *(Pause.)* My purpose here was to defeat Telemann. Now I can accomplish only the opposite, affixing to my name, for all time, the moniker *second choice*. Instead, I shall return to Darmstadt and await my next chance to face him. And I shall not leave empty-handed. Before I left, I secured from my employers a promise that they would double my salary to keep me!

FASCH *(Beat.)* Yes, well done, Graupner.

KAUFMANN Oh, very amusing! For *we* know, though he does not, that Telemann has employed precisely the same strategy, with superior results!

GRAUPNER *(Beat.)* He did what? *(Pause.)* Damn. *(Quietly, to himself.)* "Think less of those who think less of you." *(He begins to walk off.)*

FASCH But . . . may *we* now enter?

SCHOTT And speak to the Council?

GRAUPNER *(Turning back.)* They have departed for the night. Through the stained glass. On the other side of the cathedral.

(GRAUPNER *leaves. A long moment. The others regard one another.*)

KAUFMANN Is this what's known as a "hiatus"?

STEINDORFF What, exactly, have I missed?

KAUFMANN Recapitulation! *(Very rapidly, miming action and characters.)* Fasch and Graupner each have letters which suggest that one of them may have been Kuhnau's personal choice for the post, and, learning this, Herr Schott attempted to strike illicit deals with both of them, bartering his support for the veracity of either letter in exchange for mastery over the Thomasschule, his repeated rejections from which having left him bitter and acrimonious. Meanwhile, Lenck's attempt to *bribe* the Council, using funds provided, wittingly by Graupner and unwittingly by Fasch, and then compounded at the tavern, was thwarted by his incompetence as a gambler, leading to a lamentation of such heartrending pathos that *this* jaded spectator found himself on the brink of tears! *(Beat.)* Oh, which is not to say that your speech, Martin, was not well delivered. It was. Yes, um . . . *fiery*. But it is less well crafted. For one thing, the loss of your music was the result of random misfortune, whereas in Lenck's case he ironically brought it about himself. Your speech also suffered as a result of its position, immediately following *another* impassioned litany.

(There is a scream from offstage. GRAUPNER *hobbles back into the room. There is an arrow piercing his thigh.* KAUFMANN *leaps up.)*

KAUFMANN Run! It's the Frothing Marauder of the Glade!

SCHOTT Kaufmann, what is the matter with you? That is clearly Graupner!

KAUFMANN Oh, yes. I assumed that after two false entrances the deranged outlaw would surely appear next.

SCHOTT Yes, well, traditionally the third entrance would be the pivotal one, but . . . (*Beat.*) What am I saying?

(*Meanwhile,* FASCH *has gone to* GRAUPNER.)

FASCH What is going on?

GRAUPNER Tremendous events! Approaching from a distance! Closing like a vise before me, blocking my egress: *soldiers!* Hundreds of them, swords drawn, arrows in flight . . . ah! Attempting to slip by, I took this wound. Which has pierced the music stitched to my thigh and soaked it in my blood! I sought sanctuary in the church, but even now they make camp on the cobblestones below! (*Beat.*) Apparently, the last man to escape the city was Herr Telemann.

FASCH Who are they?

GRAUPNER Half of them wear the livery of Zwickau, and the rest carry the banners of Merseburg. But they are allied together! Forces joined against a common enemy!

FASCH Who?

GRAUPNER The sole culprit behind the heated exchange of provocative letters.

FASCH The heated exch—

GRAUPNER Yes! Apparently, it was the work of a single adept calligraphist, and now he has been traced . . . to here!

LENCK (*Beat.*) He has?

GRAUPNER His final letter was unsigned, but it bore the unmistakably genuine seal of the Leipzig Guild of Musicians.

SCHOTT (*Beat.*) The what?

GRAUPNER And it revealed a lecherous affair between the

wife of Merseburg's ambassador and the son of Zwikau's lord.

STEINDORFF (*Beat.*) Did it?

GRAUPNER And so, until the guilty party surrenders, the armies will lay siege. And fire upon any organist answering to the name Georg! Or Johann!

(KAUFMANN *applauds the obvious climax, then hesitates.*)

KAUFMANN The wife of Merseburg's ambassador, did you say?

GRAUPNER Yes. Gisela by name.

KAUFMANN Oh, I see. (*Pause.*) Well, thank goodness this is only a play!

(*There is a pounding at the door of the church: three slow echoing crashes. The men look toward the sound. A moment.*)

GRAUPNER They are here.

(KAUFMANN *takes a step toward the door. He looks around at the others. He goes to* GRAUPNER *and touches the wound, raising fingers covered with blood.*)

KAUFMANN Oh. (*Pause.*) Oh! I . . . I see!

GRAUPNER I'm not wounded badly.

KAUFMANN But I am! Oh, Gisela . . . The Unbelievably Credulous Fool is . . . me.

(*From outside, the sound of drums.*)

SCHOTT How appropriate. The Thomaskirche is besieged.

(*Blackout. The sound of drums continues.*)

Seven

(*The anteroom, hours later. The sound of drums.* GRAUPNER, *his wound dressed, lies unconscious in the center of the room.* STEINDORFF *enters, fleeing. Exhausted, he leans for a moment against one wall.* KAUFMANN *enters in pursuit, sword drawn.*)

STEINDORFF Friedrich, there is no need for this.
KAUFMANN I shall sever every part of you that has touched my Gisela.
STEINDORFF Ahh!

(KAUFMANN *attacks. They exchange a few blows.* STEINDORFF *flees.* KAUFMANN *pursues.* SCHOTT *enters. He is carrying a hammer. He pauses for a moment in the center of the room as he gazes at the double doors. Then, hearing approaching footsteps, he ducks through an exit and out of view.* LENCK *enters, sword drawn. He is dressed as a nursemaid. He looks around warily.* STEINDORFF *enters and spots* LENCK.)

STEINDORFF Oh, Lenck, thank goodness, I'm . . . (*Beat.*) What on earth are you wearing?
LENCK It's the only clothing I have left.
STEINDORFF No matter. He's gone mad. And is, for the moment, hopelessly lost among the vestibules. Save me! All debts between us will be canceled!
LENCK Yes. (*Pause.*) It is time to cancel the debts between us.
STEINDORFF (*Beat.*) What?

LENCK At last my father the wheelwright shall be avenged!

STEINDORFF *(Beat.)* Your . . . ? But . . . ! Ahh!

(LENCK *attacks. They exchange a few blows.* STEINDORFF *flees.* LENCK *pursues.* SCHOTT *reenters and walks toward the double doors.* FASCH *enters, kneels by* GRAUPNER, *and searches his pockets. He sees* SCHOTT.)

FASCH Herr Schott.

SCHOTT Fasch. What are you doing?

FASCH I gave my opium to Graupner for his pain. Now I cannot sleep. *(Beat.)* Is that a hammer?

SCHOTT What? This? Yes. Yes, it is.

FASCH What for?

SCHOTT So that I might . . . lodge a protest! Yes. Against the unfairness of the audition! In the form of ninety-five theses! To be nailed here, to the great doors of the Thomaskirche itself!

FASCH Where is this document?

SCHOTT Naturally, I cannot show it to you.

FASCH *(Beat.)* You're here to destroy the organ.

SCHOTT That is absurd.

(FASCH *has moved to block the door.*)

FASCH Yes, it is. This is a time for solidarity, not for violence.

(STEINDORFF *stumbles in.*)

STEINDORFF Help me!

(STEINDORFF *flees off the other side.* LENCK *and* KAUFMANN *enter in pursuit.*)

LENCK (*As he passes.*) It's the only clothing I have left.

(LENCK *and* KAUFMANN *run off.*)

FASCH What is happening here?

SCHOTT War! The threat from outside has absolved us of responsibility.

FASCH Chaos, Balthasar? From you? Surely, as a devout Lutheran—

SCHOTT Oh, but we are not Lutherans. Not tonight. Tonight we are Pietists.

FASCH You are *animals*.

SCHOTT That is what I said. And who are you to disapprove? You, too, are a carrion crow on Kuhnau's corpse. Now let me pass.

FASCH No. My purpose here is as a bulwark. Kuhnau needs me to protect him.

SCHOTT Oh. Your letter.

FASCH Yes!

SCHOTT Fasch, it is a forgery.

FASCH You cannot know that

SCHOTT I can! For I wrote it! And I sent it!

FASCH (*Pause.*) *What?*

SCHOTT (*Circling, spinning a web.*) Kuhnau hoped to guide events posthumously, yes. He would write, he said, to his most cherished pupil. A man called Johann. And so I wrote you first. An encoded melody: "Johann, I wish never to see you again. Stay out of my sight, forever. No matter what else you might hear from me in the future. Yours, Johann."

FASCH But that is not what it said.

SCHOTT That is *also* what it said. Quite by accident, you see, I created a crab canon. The piece can be read just as easily backward and upside down. Until you showed me my own letter this afternoon I had no idea why you'd come. But then I saw: I myself inadvertently summoned you here.

FASCH But . . . Kuhnau did . . . *plan* . . . to write to me?

SCHOTT No. He wrote to Graupner. Another pupil. Another Johann.

FASCH "You . . . Johann . . . are my most cherished . . ."

SCHOTT So it is settled, Fasch! We have no quarrel. You may let me by.

FASCH No. No, whether he wrote to me or not, I must . . . I must believe that he wanted me back. *I must believe it!*

SCHOTT Blind faith, Fasch? From you? You must let it go. We both must. Let us cross this threshold together. Then, Fasch, then! The mu—!

(FASCH *smashes* SCHOTT *across the face.* SCHOTT *reels and falls.*)

SCHOTT Oh! I think I swallowed my music. (*Pause.*) So be it.

(SCHOTT *draws his sword.* FASCH *draws his.* STEINDORFF *runs in, pursued by* KAUFMANN. LENCK *enters from the other side.* STEINDORFF *is trapped. Seeing* FASCH *and* SCHOTT, *the others cry out, startled.* GRAUPNER *wakes up with a cry. Everyone screams.* GRAUPNER *looks around and sees a ring of five swords.*)

GRAUPNER (*Beat.*) What on earth is going on?

(*The fight begins in earnest.* FASCH *fights* SCHOTT, STEINDORFF *fights* KAUFMANN *and* LENCK, *while* GRAUPNER, *caught, fends off wayward blows. The combat rages all over: benches and candelabras overturned, and so on. And, at its peak,* SCHOTT *runs* FASCH *through, pinning him to the double doors, through the chest.* FASCH *slides to the floor.* STEINDORFF's *sword is dashed from his hand, and death strokes from* KAUFMANN *and* LENCK *loom over him.* SCHOTT *heaves* FASCH *aside, seizes the handles, and triumphantly flings the doors wide. A great flood of sound emerges.* SCHOTT *stands framed in the doorway as the music washes over him. It is the climax of a six-voice fugue by Bach. Everyone freezes.)*

SCHOTT My God. What is it?
LENCK It's a fugue. You can hear the subject. And its
    counterpoint.
STEINDORFF And there are three voices at least.
KAUFMANN No, no. There are four.
GRAUPNER Wait. No. There, in the bass: it's five.

(The fugue cadences and fades.)

FASCH You're all quite mistaken. There were six.

*(*FASCH *collapses.* SCHOTT *remembers himself. He kneels beside* FASCH.*)*

SCHOTT Oh! Oh, Fasch, what have I done? *(Pause.)*
    Friedrich? *(He looks around wildly at the others.)* I . . . I felt
    I had no . . . This was . . . This has been . . . *predestined,*
    you see, it . . . I cannot be held resp . . . Oh, God. Oh,
    God.

*(*SCHOTT *stands. He begins to walk off, toward the outside.)*

KAUFMANN Balthasar, they will kill you!
SCHOTT I must be judged. For my crime.

*(*SCHOTT *walks slowly off. There is a long, long pause. The others cannot look at one another. Some sit. Others begin to speak, and then stop. Then* SCHOTT *runs back in.)*

SCHOTT A miracle! The armies have departed. One soldier
    alone remained, and only to bring us this message. *(He*

reads a note.) "We cannot kill a man capable of producing such beauty. Whatever he has done."

LENCK I don't understand.

GRAUPNER How did he quell and banish two armies with so little music?

FASCH *(Stirring.)* No, don't you see?

(The others react, startled, relieved.)

FASCH It's all right. I'm all right. The metal case around Schott's forged letter from Kuhnau caught the blade. I was only winded. *(Beat.)* Don't you see? He has been playing all along. For hours. We alone did not hear him. It is only clear, after all, from a greater distance. *(Pause.)* Who *was* that?

SCHOTT It was Johann.

FASCH You're going to have to be far, far more specific.

SCHOTT It was Johann Sebastian Bach.

STEINDORFF Bach, did you say? I have something of his. *(Producing a crumpled letter from his rags.)* It's a letter he wrote to his wife. I found it tied to the ankle of the messenger pigeon I was forced to kill and eat in the forest. *(Reading.)* "Leipzig. June, 1722. Darling Anna."

FASCH Half the organist's wives in Germany are called Anna.

STEINDORFF "The audition begins in the morning. But the outcome is inevitable. Herr Telemann is here, and it is clear in every way—his gait, his bearing, his gorgeous speaking voice—that he will be victorious. I'll be home in no time at all. Yours, Johann Sebastian Bach."

SCHOTT This tells us nothing. What sort of man can write . . . the music he can write?

KAUFMANN Born in Thuringia, 1685. At eight he lost his mother, and at ten was orphaned when his father died as well. In 1708, he took employment as Konzertmeister at

Weimar, and, upon the death of Weimar's Kappelmeister, Bach sought the post, only to see it offered to Georg Phillip Telemann. He then pursued a position at Cöthen, only to find himself, as a result, thrown into prison for a month by Weimar's duke. When he was released, and ensconced at Cöthen, his wife, Maria, died. Just as two of their seven children had before her. He has since remarried, and has come to Leipzig, to audition here. He brought with him his collected organ works, the title page of which bears the following inscription: "To the highest God alone to praise him, *and* to my neighbor, for his self-instruction."

STEINDORFF The account is incomplete. (*Beat.*) I only mean: Herr Bach does not know it yet, otherwise occupied as he is, but tonight he has had several more sons.

(SCHOTT, FASCH, *and then the others all turn out into pools of light. As their letters complete, the others move, fade, and vanish, until only* FASCH *and* SCHOTT *remain.*)

SCHOTT Leipzig.
FASCH June, 1722.
SCHOTT Herr Kuhnau, he began to play again.
FASCH Anna, it went on all night.
SCHOTT A prelude, in every key, with no fixed structure whatsoever.
FASCH (*Overlapping on "structure."*) A fugue, in every key, of almost mathematical perfection.
SCHOTT (*Overlapping on "mathematical."*) He played concerti in the Italian style, which seemed to summon God, a combination I heretofore would have thought impossible, and yet I heard it, unmistakably, with my own ears, along with suites in the English style, dances in the French, a Tocatta in D Minor with an opening melody that seemed to spring fresh from some dark realm of the imagination,

and all these were secular, improvisatory, and yet they contained every sacredness, every holy moment I had ever hoped to achieve when writing music of my own. And I thought to myself, Never in my life have I been proved so wrong, and never in my life have I felt so happy. Is this what you meant? Is this what I lack? Then I am in good company. For what I heard tonight is the rarest of things.

FASCH *(Overlapping on "God.")* I heard a St. Matthew Passion, and a cycle of cantatas sufficient to fill three years of Sundays, and the stories they told lived in the rise and fall of every single note, an achievement I can scarcely fathom, and yet can no longer deny, along with a Passacaglia in C Minor in which a single theme, through a miracle of formal repetition, opened outward to infinity, and all these were devotional, or rigorous, or both, but rather than being limited they felt limitless. They suggested every yearning beyond articulation I have ever hoped to summon in the music I write myself, and I thought, Never have I been so humbled, and never so moved. I will return to you, and to our daughter, a changed man.

GRAUPNER *(Overlapping on "stories.")*

Darmstadt. February, 1723.

Doctor Schultz:

   I am not, it seems, the second-greatest organist in Germany but, rather, the third-greatest. And yet, for reasons I cannot explain, this new fate sits with me better than the old one ever did. Therefore, with deep gratitude for all the help you have given me lo these many years, I hereby propose that we discontinue our sessions. Or, if not, that we perhaps begin to spend some of our time together discussing a variety of other issues that sometimes trouble me. Though, of course, if Telemann's name happens to crop up, in an organic fashion, we may discuss him. Should the need arise.

Yours, *Johann Christoph Graupner*

STEINDORFF *(Overlapping on "second-greatest.")*

Quedlinberg. March, 1728.

Father:

Please, stop your entreaties. Escaping from your house was not only the wisest decision of my life so far but, I have come to understand, the only decision of my life so far. I have carved out for myself a life here, whittled it, shaped it. I see now that the Steindorff line is inbred, stagnant. Whereas better and better wheels continue to spin themselves out of the forest where I, as a child, was seldom permitted to go. Do not write to me again.

Yours, *Johann Martin Steindorff*

LENCK *(Overlapping on "house.")*

Zwickau. September, 1736.

Catherina:

Glorious news! Pack your belongings as quickly as possible, leave Laucha, and join me here where, at last, I have a title worthy of you, and where we can finally be married. Never again will I have to dress as a woman. Except in the event that you would like me to do so, for some reason. I'm only suggesting that I wouldn't mind too terribly.

Yours, *Georg Lenck*

KAUFMANN *(Overlapping on "belongings.")*

Merseburg. April, 1743.

Gisela:

My serpent. Are any of our children really my own? I ask because, on several recent visits, I have noticed characteristics that suggest other parentage. For example, now that he has come of age, I notice that young Andreas appears to be partly Chinese. Please explain.

Yours, *Georg Friedrich Kaufmann*

FASCH *(Continuous.)*

Zerbst. November, 1748.

Herr Schott:

I have received your letter and accept your invitation.
And, of course, I would relish the opportunity to visit with
him. But it may take time to arrange the journey.

SCHOTT *(Continuous.)*

Leipzig. May, 1749.

I look forward to your arrival. And do come soon,
Fasch. After all, he won't wait forever.

FASCH *(Pause.)* Leipzig. July, 1750.

Epilogue: Da Capo

(The anteroom. FASCH *stands here, stooped with age.* SCHOTT, *as we first saw him, is seated in a chair before the doors.)*

FASCH Georg Balthasar Schott.

SCHOTT Johann Friedrich Fasch! You've come at last!

FASCH I was delighted to receive your invitation! How is the Neuekirche?

SCHOTT Fine, fine! Though my duties have expanded somewhat. *He* has been kind enough to place me in charge of the students at the Thomasschule.

FASCH From the tavern across the street, I thought I could hear *him* playing.

SCHOTT It only looks like a tavern. Now it's a music shop. But you are correct: he plays every day at this time.

FASCH The people must consider themselves blessed.

SCHOTT On the contrary, they consider themselves rationalists.

FASCH Yes. A new age is dawning.

SCHOTT No, it dawned thirty years ago, only we didn't notice. One marches boldly forward only to learn, after the fact, that one was facing the wrong direction. People now have little interest in music *or* religion. I do not know what they will call *this* age, but its chief characteristic seems to be a profound lack of enlightenment.

FASCH But *you* listen. You must.

SCHOTT Oh, yes, but . . . My favorite moments come not *while* he is playing but just *after*. I feel happiest as his final chords begin to fade to the high stone ceiling. What do you make of that?

FASCH No doubt the silence that follows seems richer than ordinary silence. Imbued, as it is, with the profound absence of the sounds you've just heard.

SCHOTT Yes . . . yes, and in it so much is clearer . . . every squeak of hinges . . . every footstep . . . Such is his mastery, I suppose: he makes even silence . . . gorgeous.

(Long pause.)

SCHOTT I was surprised not to see you at Graupner's funeral.

FASCH Graupner is dead? I received no word.

SCHOTT Oh, it was a small affair. The budget for such things had been greatly sapped by Telemann's funeral, two days earlier. (Pause.) I arrived in time to speak with him before he passed. And on his deathbed he revealed to me that he had altered his letter from Kuhnau, shifting its key signature from minor to major in order to hide its true meaning. Kuhnau, you see, had demanded that no one replace him at all! That Leipzig remain, after his death, forever without music! And that, as an eternal reminder, an urn containing his ashes be placed upon the silent organ. He even had the urn ready: a gray vase, adorned with a spiderweb of cracks, he'd received as a gift, he said, years before. From his only son. He was obviously mad: the man was childless, you see. (Pause.) Almost heartbreaking. Isn't it?

FASCH Yes. Almost.

SCHOTT He even vowed that if attempts were made to replace him he'd haunt the road to Leipzig, as a vengeful spirit. (Beat.) Ridiculous.

FASCH Yes. (Pause.) May I go inside?

SCHOTT I insist.

FASCH Do you think he's nearly finished?

SCHOTT No. Oh, no.

FASCH Do you suppose he'd mind if I just stood in the
doorway?

SCHOTT *(With deep melancholy.)* I have spent the better part of
my life in this doorway. No one has ever minded. *(Pause.)*
He will be pleased to see you. In fact, that has only just now
become possible. These last few months he has been quite
blind but, just this morning, his sight has returned!

*(FASCH, alarmed, opens the door. A simple melody, played on the
organ, floats out.)*

FASCH My word!

SCHOTT Yes, astonishing, isn't it? And at his age.

FASCH No. Oh, no. He's collapsed.

*(And now the piece is joined by other instruments—strings,
woodwinds—ghostlike.)*

SCHOTT What are you talking about? Listen to him play!

FASCH He's not moving. Herr Bach, are you all right? Herr
Bach! *Herr Bach!*

*(FASCH disappears inside the doors, while, from every direction,
from the very air, more and more instruments join, an entire
orchestra, a choir, swelling and swelling.)*

SCHOTT Fasch, don't you hear that? It's beautiful!

(FASCH emerges. What he says is nearly inaudible.)

FASCH Fetch the doctor. Quickly, go!

SCHOTT *(To be heard over the music.)* What?

FASCH Fetch the doctor! Quickly! Go, now! Go!

(FASCH *darts inside the doors and disappears.*)

SCHOTT I'm sorry, my friend, I can't hear you! You'll have to
wait for him to finish playing!

(SCHOTT *is alone, listening blissfully, eyes shut, to the music,
which builds and builds as the lights fade. He is swallowed by
darkness and sound. Fade to black.*)

Appendix: Music Specifications

1. ACT ONE, SCENE ONE. The Prelude in A Minor referred to here is specifically BWV 543. I suggest this piece mainly because it is the prelude that precedes the fugue in A minor that is required for the top of the second act. But I also like its suggestion of dark undercurrents and its sense of forward momentum.

2. ACT TWO, SCENE ONE. The Fugue in A Minor referred to here is the companion to the prelude above, and the text of Fasch's speech is actually timed to a specific recording, by E. Power Biggs. In his rendition, the Second Voice enters at 0:13, and the Third just before 0:38. The first cadence at which the music fades is at 1:08, and it's really not much of a cadence. When the music continues as Fasch talks about the Fourth and Fifth Voices, it can begin exactly where it left off. Here, Fasch's description no longer matches the piece exactly—for one thing, this piece never becomes a Six Voice fugue. But there is a reentry of the theme here that does sound like it might be the introduction of a pair of new voices. And when Fasch refers to "returning to your theme," the theme does, in fact, ring out high above the other voices. If the music simply continues to play under Fasch, through Graupner's entrance, it will enter a long development section in a major key that will mirror what Fasch says about fugal devices. There is no need for a cadence when the music next fades, and it can simply do so whenever Fasch reaches that point in the speech. When the music reenters

for the climax, it should do so at a point late enough in the piece that the end of the fugue will accompany the reprise of the end of the first act.

3. ACT TWO, SCENE SEVEN. It has proven very hard to find the right piece to use for the moment that stops the sword fight. It's important that the piece climax and fade relatively soon after the doors open, and that the music be, of course, breathtaking. But the ends of fugues, even very complicated ones, even Bach's, tend not to sound particularly complicated: they are usually just a series of chords. And an intricate section from the middle of a fugue won't cadence. Be prepared to try many different options in tech.

4. EPILOGUE. The final music cue is incredibly important, and there has been confusion in the past about what the stage directions actually mean. When Fasch opens the door, we should hear a simple *melody* played on the organ, *not* a reprise of the drone from the end of the first scene. It should sound like someone is actually playing. Then, when Fasch says that Bach has collapsed, there is a disjunction between what we hear and what Fasch sees: that's the point. Only then is the organ joined by other instruments, strings, woodwinds, a choir, etc., perhaps coming not simply from inside the doors, but from everywhere, swelling, until the scene is swallowed. Fasch sees one reality. Schott, and the audience, hear another.

History in *Bach at Leipzig*

The Leipzig audition really took place.

In 1722, Johann Kuhnau, who really was organist at the Thomaskirche and master of the Thomasschule, really did die. The Leipzig Council did invite organists from across Germany to audition for the vacant post. The organists in the play in fact represent, or at any rate have the same names as, nearly all of the actual candidates.*

Telemann really was the first choice for the post, and really did use the offer as leverage to negotiate for better terms at Hamburg. Graupner, who, like Fasch, really had been a student at the Thomasschule, really was the second choice for the post, but found himself unable to secure his release from his employment at Darmstadt. And so, of course, the victory went to Bach, who really did remain in Leipzig until his death in 1750.

Just about everything else is made up.

*The other two were Christian Friedrich Rolle and Andreas Christoph Duve. They have been excluded from the play for what should be an obvious reason.